INSTRUCTOR'S MANUAL TO ACCOMPANY

FILM ART

AN INTRODUCTION • FIFTH EDITION

DAVID BORDWELL
KRISTIN THOMPSON

University of Wisconsin

D1108931

The McGraw-Hill Companies, Inc.

New York   St. Louis   San Francisco   Auckland   Bogotá
Caracas   Lisbon   London   Madrid   Mexico City   Milan   Montreal
New Delhi   San Juan   Singapore   Sydney   Tokyo   Toronto

McGraw-Hill
A Division of The McGraw·Hill Companies

Instructor's Manual to Accompany
FILM ART: An Introduction, Fifth Edition

ISBN 0-07-006635-3

1 2 3 4 5 6 7 8 9 0 BKM BKM 9 0 9 8 7 6

Contents

PART ONE

ORGANIZATION AND TEACHING STRATEGIES

PART TWO

CHAPTER-BY-CHAPTER GUIDE TO FILM ART: AN INTRODUCTION

PART THREE

MAKING SLIDES/USEFUL ADDRESSES

CONTENTS

INTRODUCTION

The Goals of the Instructor's Manual

This manual offers general suggestions for an approach to organizing a semester based on the textbook <u>Film Art: An Introduction</u>, as well as specific recommendations for lecturing, leading discussions, and assigning papers on the topics discussed in each chapter of <u>Film Art</u>. In addition, we offer a bank of test questions appropriate to each chapters (with the exception of Chapter Eleven, the Sample Analyses, which are oriented toward the assignment of term papers). You may wish to choose the films for weekly screening to tally closely with the major examples for each chapter (e.g., showing <u>Grand Illusion</u> the week you teach cinematography). Alternatively, you may wish to have your students see an entirely new example in the screening. Thus we also offer a small selection of suggestions of appropriate films that could be shown to illustrate each chapter. In some cases, we suggest films for one chapter that will also be mentioned in a later chapter (e.g., <u>Jules and Jim</u> could be shown for Chapter Three, "The Significance of Film Form," but it is also analyzed briefly in Chapter Nine, on film sound).

The manual is presented in three parts. This introduction offers general suggestions for organizing a course designed to introduce students to the basics of film aesthetics. It also offers some general tips for dealing with specific aspects of such a course. The second part constitutes the bulk of the book. There we describe <u>Film Art</u> chapter by chapter, suggesting ways to teach each, including examination questions. The final section describes methods for making slides from film frames and video images for use as examples during lectures. These slides are also very helpful for presenting essay questions during tests. This section ends with some helpful addresses.

Bibliographic Sources

For the most part, we have avoided giving extensive bibliographical citations in this manual, since most of the basic sources relating to each chapter are listed in the "Notes & Queries" sections in _Film Art_ and in the bibliography for Chapter Twelve. In a few other cases we have provided a small number of additional bibliographic references.

PART ONE

ORGANIZATION AND TEACHING STRATEGIES

Teaching Film Art

Organizing a Syllabus

The organization of introductory film courses varies enormously, of course, depending on such factors as whether your school is on a semester or quarter system and how many lectures you give a week. A common way of teach film courses is to have two one-hour lectures per week, with a screening of one feature film followed by a one-hour discussion section led by yourself and/or teaching assistants. In our descriptions of teaching methods we shall assume something close to this model, but we hope that our suggestions can easily be adapted to your individual circumstances.

In a standard semester of around 14 weeks, the most straightforward way of teaching Film Art would be to teach one chapter per week, showing a feature film (ideally along with occasional short films) to illustrate each. This would leave a week or two free for examinations or paper due-dates. If you have the luxury of devoting two semesters to any one topic, it should probably be Chapter Seven, on cinematography, since that is the longest single chapter on basic techniques.

There are other ways to lay out the course. You may wish to emphasize film history; the discussion of teaching Chapter Twelve gives suggestions on how to do that. Another approach is to teach the chapters in a different order, emphasizing film techniques and then moving on to film form. The sample analyses in Chapter Eleven could be made an integral part of the course if you choose to show some of the films discussed there; alternatively, the sample analyses can provide models for term papers if you wish to assign a close study of a single film as a term paper.

The Use of Visual Examples

Most film classes depend on the extensive use of visual examples, in the form of both slides and clips. We aim here to suggest how such teaching aids can be used in classes, examinations, and paper assignments. In the third part of this manual, we include a section on how to make slides of actual film frames, whether from 16mm or 35mm copies of films or from the video screen. Making such slides takes work, but once they are made, they can offer examples for your classes for years to come, and they make it possible to formulate exam questions that closely test your students' abilities to recognize specific film techniques.

Screening Notes

Students coming into their first film course often do not realize how difficult it is to remember what they see when watching a movie. They are used to watching films as casual entertainment. Thus when they find themselves expected to analyze what they have seen in a class discussion and even to answer exam questions concerning a film, they may be frustrated by their inability to remember specific scenes or the order in which the action occurred.

It is useful during the first class session to tell them to take notes as they watch the screenings--and to learn to do this without looking away from the screen. This is a difficult skill that any good film student must master (though it does take a bit of practice--and no flashlights allowed, as this would disturb fellow viewers and encourage the one with the flashlight to look away from the screen). Learning to run a finger along the edge of the notebook or even using a ruler to guide the pen helps prevent one from writing over previous notes. Some teachers require that their students keep a viewing diary, to be inspected at intervals through the course. Some students may grumble about taking notes, but it will help them immeasurably.

Students should write down the techniques they observe, the important plot points, and anything that occurs to them that is relevant to the subject being studied that week. Even a simple running description can act as a memory aid.

One way to encourage and guide note-taking

during the film is to provide a "study guide" for each screening. This could consist of an abbreviated credits list, the film's date and running time, and one or two questions which the students can glance over before the film starts. The questions can point them toward things to be noticed while watching the film, and the students can start to take the notes on the sheet itself and follow onto regular blank notebook paper. The questions can also be used to kick off discussion in small-group sections. A sample study guide is provided on the next page. (It is designed to be used in Chapter Two, "Types of Films.")

4

Aliens (1986)

Credits: Director, James Cameron; written by James Cameron; edited by Ray Lovejoy; cinematography by Adrian Biddle; music by James Horner.
    Cast: Riply (Sigourney Weaver), Newt (Carrie Henn), Corporal Hicks (Michael Biehn), Cameron Burke (Paul Reisner), Private Vasquez (Jenette Goldstein), Bishop (Lance Henriksen), Lieutenant Gorman (William Hope), Hudson (Bill Paxson).

Study Questions

1.   Aliens is simultaneously a horror film, a science-fiction film, and a war film. What conventions of these three genres are used in the film?

2.   How does this mix of conventional genres create innovations in Aliens?

Unfamiliar Kinds of Films

Students often complain if they are made to watch films that are not the sort that they are used to. Black-and-white, subtitled, and silent films are often a challenge to them. You can reduce such complaints with some simple strategies. First, be candid about what types of films will be shown and also about the fact that no student will like all the films that will be shown in the class (just as he or she would probably not like all the books assigned in a literature course). The point of the course is not to entertain them or to show them only the sorts of films they are already used to watching. Rather, the point is to expand their horizons and teach them something about the wide range of films available to them. Watching unfamiliar films is a requirement of the course, and if this is made clear from the start, you will probably meet with less resistence.

Another helpful tactic (preferably used in conjunction with the previous one) is to arrange your syllabus to ease the students gradually into the more unfamiliar sorts of films. You might begin with a color, sound film in English, then progress to a black-and-white film in English, a silent film, a color film with subtitles, or some sequence of this sort. The rest of the semester could then provide a variety of types of film. Some students will always be resistent to new experiences, but others will be grateful to you for having helped them discover unsuspected possibilities in the cinema.

The Examples Used in **Film Art**

Film Art contains an enormous number of illustrations of the various film techniques described. In choosing these, we have tried to do exactly what we have just described: to introduce your students to the enormous range of types of films that have been made in all periods. We refer to everything from the early short films of the pre-1900 period to the most recent Hollywood films. We include frame enlargements from films of Third World countries, European countries, and independent filmmakers in the US. Most students, like most viewers in the US, have watched mainly one type of film for most of their lives. We aim to provide a glimpse of the enormous variety of the cinema.

Using Slides and Clips in Examinations

When testing students on the art of the cinema, it is extremely helpful to be able to use visual aids for some questions--especially essay questions. The four chapters on techniques (Six through Nine) cry out for this treatment. Even a small collection of slides and clips, if well planned, will permit you to ask for reasonably detailed essays.

If you show clips during exams, you should suggest that your students take notes during the screenings of the clips. (Back covers of standard exam booklets are useful for this purpose.) This will help them give more precise analyses in their essays.

The "Notes and Queries"

Each chapter of Film Art ends with a "Notes and Queries" section. These are intended to make the teaching of Film Art more flexible. They serve several functions. First, they offer you basic bibliography and suggestions for lecture topics. Second, if you are teaching a large lecture course and have some eager or advanced students, the Notes and Queries give you a way of directing them to further inquiry into film, particularly term papers. Third, if you are teaching upper-level students, the Notes and Queries again offer starting points for term papers. Thus Film Art is designed to be both an introductory and intermediate textbook.

Dealing with Complaints about Grades

As in other subjects, some students in film courses complain about the grades they receive. It is often difficult to explain to them why they have not done as well as they had hoped. We have found it helpful to make photocopies of a sampling of the best tests and papers we have received (with the consent of the students who wrote them). These can be kept on file and shown to students who seek to improve their performance. Once they read this A-level work, they realize that you are comparing them to the the best actual work of their classmates and not to some abstract ideal. This tactic also gives them a notion of what can be accomplished by their dedicated peers; success in your course becomes a more plausible goal.

Examination Questions

This manual contains a test bank for each chapter, averaging about thirty questions for each. The exception is Chapter Eleven, the Sample Analyses. These are intended for use in relation to discussion and/or paper assignments, and we assume that you will not be testing on them. The questions are generally given in the objective multiple-choice and true/false formats, with a few essay questions at the end.

You may wish to give pop quizzes, using relatively simple questions, to make sure your students are doing the assigned reading. We have marked those examination questions that we feel would also be appropriate for pop quizzes with a > in the left margin.

In some cases we have asked questions concerning the filmic examples used in <u>Film Art</u> (e.g., the precise graphic matches in the work of Yasujiro Ozu or the four repeated shots with different soundtracks from <u>Letter from Siberia</u>). The textbook's purpose is primarily to teach students how better to understand the aesthetic qualities of the films they watch. But an important secondary purpose is to expose them to a wide range of important films of various types. By the end of the course, they should be aware of some of the major films and filmmakers.

We do not expect the students to remember every film mentioned, and we have asked questions only on those films that serve as major examples, i.e., those for which illustrations are provided or which serve as the primary example of a given technique or which are mentioned more than once in a chapter. (For example, in Chapter Nine an entire page is devoted to five frame enlargements and two paragraphs describing an important example of offscreen sound in <u>Stagecoach</u>, and we have included a question on that subject in the test bank.) If you decide to use some of these questions, you might wish to tell the students this at the beginning of the course. That will have the advantage of encouraging them to study the illustrations more closely.

Similarly, if you plan to draw heavily upon our test-bank questions, you might want to point out early in the course that the Glossary at the back of <u>Film Art</u> lists many of the crucial terms and concepts discussed in the book and thus acts almost as an index to material that will be on the exams. This should lead them to use the Glossary more frequently and help them learn better. It also should help you answer the inevitable question, "What's going to be on the exam?"

We have assumed that you will not necessarily use all of the exam questions but will pick and choose among them. You may not want to use every question exactly as we have written it, but we hope that each would provide a useful starting point for revision. Please note that in a few cases the phrasing of one question in a chapter's test bank may hint at the answer to another question in the same test bank.

PART TWO

CHAPTER-BY-CHAPTER GUIDE TO FILM ART: AN INTRODUCTION

CHAPTER ONE

THE WORK OF FILM PRODUCTION

Chapter Outline

Technical Factors in Film Production
Social Factors in Film Production
Modes of Production: The Studio Process
The Preproduction Phase
The Production Phase
Postproduction
Independent Production
Modes of Production: Individual and Collective
Implications of Different Modes of Film Production
After Production: Distribution and Exhibition
Film and Video
Notes and Queries
The Illusion of Movement in the Cinema
The Technical Basis of Cinema
Modes of Film Production
Production Stills Versus Frame Enlargements
Authorship
Film and Video

Teaching "The Work of Film Production"

The Purpose of the Chapter

Why include a unit on film production in a course on basic film appreciation? _Film Art_ is not intended to teach students how to make films (though it is occasionally used in introductory filmmaking classes). Rather, Chapter One is designed to get students thinking about films as _made_ objects.

Most people have some passing awareness of film production. In recent years, short documentaries on the making of various movies have been used for advertising purposes, and the spread of "infotainment" programs on cable television has meant that behind-the-scenes footage and inter- views with filmmakers are increasingly used to publicize new releases. But most viewers probably tend to forget such information when they are actually caught up in the viewing experience.

Moreover, many basic facts about filmmaking do not receive attention in behind-the-scenes glimpses. For example, many people assume that all the scenes in films are made using several cameras; in reality, most scenes are put together from shots taken by the same camera, moved to different places in the setting. Only when one realizes this fact do the complexities of conti- nuity editing and sound mixing become apparent.

By learning such facts, students can start from the beginning of the course to think about the various techniques that go into filmmaking. They can become aware that the filmmakers have an enormous variety of possibilities open to them and constantly make choices. Thus later in the semes- ter, when they study the chapters on individual film techniques (mise-en-scene, cinematography, editing, and sound), students may be better pre- pared to see them as functioning as part of a larger system, the film as a unified construct.

A Lecture from a Filmmaker

We tend to think of filmmakers as working on feature films in large cities, but there are many kinds of filmmakers all over the country. Even if your school is not in a city, your town or one nearby is likely to have firms making advertise- ments, instructional documentaries, or animated films. Your own teaching institution may have filmmaking courses or a television station with staffs of specialists. As we describe in <u>Film Art</u>, the same basic stages of production and series of tasks are used in many different types of films. Filmmakers are often happy to lecture on their craft, and it may even be possible to arrange for your students to tour a film facility and see how equipment, like editing stations and sound mixing boards, is used.

Teaching a Case Study

One useful way to teach Chapter One is to undertake a case study. That is, you can show a film and lecture and/or assign a reading on the making of that film. There are an increasing number of books and articles available that detail the backgrounds of major films, focusing in part on the work of the production workers that are described in Chapter One.

For example, Rudy Behlmer's <u>America's Favorite Movies: Behind the Scenes</u> (New York: Frederick Ungar, 1982) contains a series of studies of the production processes for several American classics. Each is concise enough to assign as a reading. The films included are: <u>Frankenstein</u> (1931), <u>Lost Horizon</u> (1937), <u>Snow White and the Seven Dwarfs</u>, <u>The Adventures of Robin Hood</u>, <u>Gunga Din</u>, <u>Stagecoach</u> (1939), <u>Casablanca</u>, <u>Laura</u>, <u>All About Even</u>, <u>A Streetcar Named Desire</u>, <u>The African Queen</u>, <u>Singin' in the Rain</u>, and <u>High Noon</u>. Other brief studies of the production backgrounds of classic films can be found in the series, "Rutgers Films in Print," currently appearing from Rutgers University Press. As of this writing there are over twenty of these volumes, covering such films as <u>Bringing Up Baby</u>, <u>Breathless</u>, and <u>The Maltese Falcon</u>. Each contains a brief production history, a shot-by-shot breakdown of the entire film, as well as a collection of reprinted essays and interviews relating to the film.

Book-length studies can be of use in preparing a lecture on a production case study. Here is a sampling of what is currently available:

Robert L. Carringer, <u>The Making of **Citizen Kane**</u> (Berkeley: The University of California Press, 1985).

Aljean Harmetz, <u>The Making of **The Wizard of Oz**</u> (New York: Limelight Books, 1984).

Aljean Harmetz, <u>Round Up the Usual Suspects: The Making of **Casablanca**--Bogart, Bergman, and World War II</u> (New York: Hyperion, 1992).

13

the 1953 Movie and Its 1983 Restoration
(New York: Knopf, 1988).
Donald Knox, The Magic Factor: How MGM Made
An American in Paris (New York: Prae-
ger, 1973).
Ed Naha, The Making of **Dune** (New York:
Berkley, 1984).
Stephen Rebello, Alfred Hitchcock and the
Making of **Psycho** (New York: Dembner,
1990).
Julie Salamon, The Devil's Candy: **The Bon-
fire of the Vanities** Goes to Hollywood
(Boston: Houghton Mifflin, 1991).
John Sayles, Thinking in Pictures: The
Making of the Movie **Matewan** (Boston:
Houghton Mifflin, 1987).

One possiblity is to begin your semester with a case study of the making of The Wizard of Oz (using the Harmetz book), since this film is also used as a major example of film form in Chapter Three.   Another is to begin with Citizen Kane (using the Carringer book), since this film is the central example in Chapter Four, on narrative form, and is further discussed in Chapter Ten, on film style.   You could then show Kane again the week you teach Chapter Four; students can benefit from two viewings of such a complex film.

Paper Assignment

You may wish to assign students to choose a recent film and write a research paper on its pro-duction (ideally from preproduction to distribu-tion).   Periodicals that regularly cover various aspects of film production include: Variety (business), American Cinematographer (case studies of cinematography), Cinefex (detailed case studies of special-effects films). Certain films obvious-ly receive more extensive coverage than others. For example, the first animated feature created entirely through computer imaging, Toy Story, was widely discussed in both the specialist and the popular press.   Increasingly, laserdiscs are becoming a source of information on the making of individual films.

Laserdisc Supplements

"Special editions" of laserdiscs often include supplementary material on the production of films. Such material includes original scripts, storyboards, behind-the-scenes photographs, costume designs, and the like. It is usually not possible to assign students to go through this material in the same way that they would read a book or article, since most supplements are assemblages of documents and images rather than narratives of films' production processes. Still, if you have facilities for showing video images in class, you might find it useful to work such material into your lectures on production. Similarly, if you wish to assign a paper for the early part of the course, you might direct your students to such laser discs as a source of information.

One of the most detailed collections of production material for a single film has been assembled by Robert Carringer for the Criterion Collection's edition of The Magnificent Ambersons (CC1109L); this includes interviews with Orson Welles, the shooting script, storyboards, the original magazine serial, the Mercury Theatre radio version, and other background material. (This disc can be especially valuable used in conjunction with Carringer's book, **The Magnificent Ambersons: A Reconstruction** [Berkeley: University of California Press, 1993].) Other laser discs with elaborate presentations of production material include: Aliens ("Special Widescreen Collector's Edition," Fox Video 1504-85); Tootsie (Criterion Collection 145), with running commentary by director Sidney Pollack and a documentary on the making of the film; Raging Bull (Criterion Collection 120), with commentary by director Martin Scorsese and editor Thelma Schoonmaker and reproductions of storyboards and the shooting script; and El Mariachi (Special Collector's Edition, Widescreen Version, Columbia 53616), with a highly entertaining commentary by director Robert Rodriguez explaining how he cut corners to make the film cheaply. Many supplements, however, are less useful, supplying only trailers and outtakes. Magazines that regularly review laser discs and describe their supplementary material include <u>Widescreen Review</u> and <u>Video Watchdog</u>. Although it is no longer published, the twenty-three issues of <u>The Perfect Vision</u> that appeared from Winter 1986/87 and October 1994 contain in-depth reviews of many laserdiscs that appeared during that period.

EXAMINATION QUESTIONS

> in the margin indicates a question suitable for use in either a pop quiz or an exam.

Multiple-choice Questions

> Which of the following is <u>not</u> one of the three modes of production?

      a.   Individual

*   b.   Conglomerate

      c.   Collective

      d.   Studio

> The assembly phase of production involves:

      a.   Casting.

      b.   Gathering of props.

*   c.   Editing.

      d.   Scouting locations.

"Critical flicker fusion" is:

      a.   The final stage in the manufacture of raw film stock.

*   b.   The flashing of film frames on a screen quickly enough to create an illusion of movement.

      c.   The ideal length of time each frame

should be exposed during filming.

    d.   The moment when the exposed image appears on the film during the developing process.

> Positive copies of films are made using which of these machines?

  *   a.   A printer

        b.   A camera

        c.   A projector

        d.   A Steadicam

"Gauge" refers to what quality of the film strip?

        a.   Its durability

        b.   Its thickness

        c.   Its total running time

  *   d.   Its width

A preliminary synopsis of a film's narrative is called a:

        a.   Blueprint.

        b.   Brief.

  *   c.   Treatment.

        d.   Try-out.

> Which of these is <u>not</u> a standard width for film strips?

        a.   16mm

  *   b.   24mm

        c.   35mm

d.　70mm

A "master shot" is:

 a.　A shot considered good enough for inclusion in a film.

 b.　A preliminary test of whether the camera is working.

* c.　A single shot of all the action of a scene.

 d.　A close view of the film's star.

> "Nonlinear editing" means:

 a.　Arrangings scenes shot "out of continuity" during production.

 b.　Editing at intervals during the shooting of a film.

* c.　Editing using video and computer.

 d.　Combining color and black-and-white footage in the same scene.

A film company is "vertically integrated" if it:

 a.　Releases more than ten films a year.

* b.　Produces, distributes, and exhibits films.

 c.　Controls all phases of production through a strong chain of command from top management downward.

 d.　Has all its personnel under long-term contract.

The "aspect ratio" of a film refers to:

 a.　The profits of a film in proportion to

its costs.

    b. The percentage of shots that are made on location.

*   c. The width of its images in relation to their height.

    d. The proportion of the total amount of footage shot to the amount used in the final cut.

An "art house" is:

    a. A film theater that also displays works of local painters and sculptors.

    b. A company that supplies real art works for use in film sets.

    c. A theater designed to resemble the "movie palaces" of the 1930s.

*   d. A theater that shows foreign-language and independent films.

> Which of these methods is <u>not</u> a method for showing theatrical films on television?

    a. Panning and scanning

    b. Colorization

    c. Time compression

*   d. Step-printing

A clapboard is:

*   a. A tool for creating sound effects in postproduction.

*   b. A sign held in front of the lens to record the number of each take.

    c. A large chart listing the personnel due

to work on a film on any given day.

    d. A device used to signal extras in large crowd scenes.

True-False Questions

<u>T</u> F A strip of film consists of base and emulsion.

T <u>F</u> It is not yet possible to use digital sound tracks for films.

<u>T</u> F The collective mode of filmmaking was most common during the 1960s and 1970s.

T <u>F</u> Cinematographers almost always use three to five cameras in shooting the action of each scene.

<u>T</u> F A storyboard is a series of drawings of the shots planned for a film.

T <u>F</u> To save money, most directors try to shoot only one take of each shot.

T <u>F</u> A film's direct sound is recorded optically during filming, then later transferred onto magnetic tape.

T <u>F</u> The typical independent film has about the same budget as a studio production.

<u>T</u> F The individual mode of filmmaking is common in documentary filmmaking.

T <u>F</u> Most exhibitors do not bother to advertise that they use stereophonic sound equipment, since research shows audience members do not select theaters on the basis of sound quality.

T <u>F</u> Film images and video images can carry about the same amount of visual information.

<u>T</u> F "Letterboxing" is a method for showing wide-

screen films on video.

T <u>F</u> A film's musical track is typically composed during the preproduction phase.

Essay Questions

Explain why the director is the person most commonly viewed as the "author" of a film.

Explain what shooting "out of continuity" means and why filmmakers would use this method.

<u>Film Art</u> describes several important differences between the medium of film and the medium of video, as well as changes that films sometimes undergo when they are shown on television or video. Discuss at least three of these differences or changes in as much detail as you can.

[Note on this question: The differences in the two media that are described in the section "Film and Video" in <u>Film Art</u> are 1) the greater amount of information carried by the film image (scan lines and pixels in video vs. silver halide grains in film), 2) film's greater contrast ratio, 3) film's better rendition of color, and 4) film's larger scale (theater screen vs. television monitor screen). The changes made in film when shown on TV are: 1) frequent changes in editing and sound, 2) time compression, and 3) alteration of aspect ratio (cropping, pan and scan).

If you choose to use this essay question, you may wish to tell the students in advance that such a question will appear on the exam.]

CHAPTER TWO

TYPES OF FILMS

Chapter Outline

Basic Types
Documentary versus Fiction
Animated Film
Experimental and Avant-Garde Film
Film Genres
The Western
The Horror Film
Notes and Queries
Basic Types of Films
On Roger and Me
Genres and Society
Specific Genres

Teaching "Types of Films"

The Purpose of the Chapter

In the first chapter, students studied how films are made by filmmakers. In this and subsequent chapters, we turn to how they are "made" in another sense--how they are composed of many elements: camera techniques, sound, motifs, character traits, and so on. Chapter Two deals with the widely recognized conventions that allow us to understand what kind of film we are watching.

The categories we discuss in Chapter Two are widely used in everyday life. Without having taken a film course, most people understand the basic difference between a documentary and a fiction film. They can recognize that an animated film is shot in a way that distinguishes it from live action. They can tell their friends that they prefer horror films to musicals. This chapter aims to lead students to think about the assumptions that allow us to make such distinctions. It also should help students realize that these types of films are not always absolutely distinct and that they may be mixed within single films. This chapter also gets students to think about the difference between narrative and non-narrative films and thus prepares them for Chapter Four, "Narrative as a Formal System" and Chapter Five, "Nonnarrative Formal Systems." Finally, it helps ease students into the analysis of films by starting with aspects that are relatively familiar to them.

The chapter falls into two large portions, examining two different ways in which we usually divide films into types. The first, "basic types," depends on our assumptions about how and with what purpose the film was made. For example, we usually assume that a documentary will tell us something factually true about the world, while a fiction film may present pure fantasy. The second category of types is genre. In thinking about genre, we are concerned less with the making and purposes of the film than with its subject matter and the conventions it shares with other, similar films. We discuss two major examples of genres: the Western and the horror film.

Teaching Basic Types of Films

Since this chapter aims to get students to examine assumptions they already hold, it ideally should be taught with a considerable amount of discussion. You might show a series of short clips from a variety of films and have the students decide into what category each falls. The discussion could then revolve around what cues in the clips led them to their conclusions. If you take this approach, you could start out with films that fall quite obviously into one category or another, then progress to some films in which there is greater ambiguity. For example, showing the credits sequence of Oliver Stone's JFK (starting just past the title) provides a vivid demonstration of the fine line between categories, as Stone begins with documentary footage and gradually mixes it with staged shots (often very difficult to distinguish from the "real thing").

The main screening could involve a film that

demonstrates the difficulties in creating hard-and-fast rules when we discuss types of films. Young Mr. Lincoln or Stone's Nixon raise the issue of why biographical films with actors are not considered documentaries. (The latter film in particular spurred an enormous amount of press debate over whether it was--or needed to be--historically accurate and educational.) Alternatively, some of the controversial documentaries mentioned in the chapter, such as Roger and Me and The Thin Blue Line, would raise similar issues from the other side. Why are the considerable manipulations of events on the parts of the film-makers not enough to disqualify these films as documentaries--or are they?

Another approach to the screening would be to put together a program of short films exemplifying the various types of films discussed. Since every film fits into one or more of these categories, we have not offered a specific list of suggested films for this area, though the "Suggested Films" sections of each chapter of this manual contain examples of all types.

Teaching Film Genre

Students come into introductory film courses possessing an extensive but unsystematic knowledge of film genres. Our goal is to make them aware of how we understand that a film belongs to a given genre and why genres might be so appealing to audiences. One approach to lecturing on the subject would be to take the basic concepts discussed in the book--conventions, iconography, and innovations--and apply them to a third genre.

Some of the standard books that might be of help in preparing such a lecture are listed in the "Notes and Queries" section of Chapter Two.

Once the students understand these concepts, you can show them a film, either in the Western or horror genres, or in the genre you discussed in lecture. Remind them to take notes on the film, especially emphasizing conventions and icons that they recognize from other films they have seen (or that were mentioned in the text or in lecture); they should also note down anything that seems

24

unusual within that genre, and discussion can touch on whether these are true innovations.

Some Possible Paper Topics

Genres are defined by common consensus rather than by firm and objectively fixed rules. Thus it might be useful for a student to read a number of books and articles on a single genre and write a comparative study of how different analysts define the same genre.

Genres are also used widely in publicity. A student might choose a few recent films from different genres and examine how reviewers, both in the popular (e.g., Entertainment Weekly) and the trade press (e.g., Variety), draw upon assumptions about genre conventions and innovations.

SUGGESTED GENRE FILMS:

Horror: Nosferatu (F. W. Murnau), The Old Dark House (James Whale), The Mummy (Karl Freund), Cat People (Jacques Tourneur), Halloween (John Carpenter)

Science Fiction: Metropolis (Fritz Lang), Invasion of the Body Snatchers (Don Siegel), The Day the Earth Stood Still (Robert Wise), Terminator 2: Judgment Day (James Cameron)

Western: Stagecoach (John Ford), My Darling Clementine (John Ford), Rio Bravo (Howard Hawks), Once Upon a Time in the West (Sergio Leone)

Musical: Footlight Parade (Lloyd Bacon), Swingtime (George Stevens), Meet Me in St. Louis (Vincente Minelli), Singin' in the Rain (Stanley Donen and Gene Kelly)

Comedy: The General (Buster Keaton and Clyde Bruckman), His Girl Friday (Howard Hawks), The King of Comedy (Martin Scorsese), Raising Arizona (Joel Coen)

Blended genres: Back to the Future Part III (Robert Zemeckis; science fiction/comedy/Western),

<u>Alien</u> (Ridley Scott; science fiction/horror), <u>Aliens</u> (James Cameron; science fiction/war), <u>Pennies from Heaven</u> (Herbert Ross; melodrama/ musical)

EXAMINATION QUESTIONS

Note: Since Chapter Two deals with concepts and conventions that are common currency among film-makers and audiences alike, it is difficult to give an extensive objective test on it. There are, for example, few new terms introduced here, and it is perhaps easier for the students, using common sense, to figure out the answers even if they have not read the chapter.

We would therefore suggest that the most effective way of testing on Chapter Two is to use essay questions, and we have provided several possibilities. If you prefer objective tests, you might either use the following multiple-choice and true-false questions as a quiz or combine these questions with some from other chapters and test on a larger portion of the book (e.g., a test on the first two chapters).

> in the margin indicates a question suitable for use in either a pop quiz or an exam.

Multiple-choice Questions

> A "direct-cinema" documentary:

    a. Is one in which the director stages the action.

*   b. Records a real event as it happens.

    c. Consists mainly of interviews with the participants in the events being docu-mented.

    d. Is made up entirely of archival footage of historic events.

"Cels" are used in drawn animation because:

26

a.   Colors show up brighter than on paper.

b.   They permit the animator to manipulate the images using a computer.

c.   They give the flat image a three-dimensional look.

*   d.   They permit different parts of the drawing to be done separately and layered together.

Stan Brakhage, Maya Deren, and Kenneth Anger are important filmmakers in the area of:

a.   Animated cinema.

b.   Documentary cinema.

*   c.   Experimental cinema.

d.   Westerns.

> A genre's "iconography" consists of:

a.   Its typical plot patterns.

b.   Its use of recurring subject matter.

c.   The sum of all its conventions.

*   d.   Its characteristic objects, settings, and stars.

> John Ford's <u>The Searchers</u> is a major example of which genre?

*   a.   The Western

b.   The detective story

c.   The science-fiction film

d.   The musical

True-False Questions

T <u>F</u> A documentary film is defined by the fact that none of the action has been staged.

<u>T</u> F "Pixillation" refers to a type of animation in which people or ordinary objects are moved frame by frame.

> T <u>F</u> Fact-based films like <u>Apollo 13</u>, <u>Schindler's List</u>, and <u>Malcolm X</u> deal with real events and are considered documentaries.

T <u>F</u> Experimental films avoid telling stories.

Essay Questions

For [title(s) of genre film(s) screened and/or discussed in class]:

1. Indicate two conventions of character, plot, theme, or iconography which are distinctive of the genre.

2. For each convention you select, show how the film[s] you select exemplify it. As evidence, cite specific scenes which use this convention.

Select any film genre we have discussed in this course. Provide two examples of conventions which are significant to the genre. Now cite two specific scenes from films which provide examples of innovative handling of those conventions.

CHAPTER THREE

THE SIGNIFICANCE OF FILM FORM

Chapter Outline

> **The Concept of Form in Film**
> > *Form as System*
> > *"Form versus Content"*
> > *Formal Expectations*
> > *Conventions and Experience*
> > *Form and Feeling*
> > *Form and Meaning*
> > *Evaluation*
>
> **Principles of Film Form**
> > *Function*
> > *Similarity and Repetition*
> > *Difference and Variation*
> > *Development*
> > *Unity/Disunity*
>
> **Notes and Queries**
> > *Form in Various Arts*
> > *The Concept of Form in Film*
> > *Form, Meaning, and Feeling*
> > *Similarity and Difference*
> > *Linear Segmentation and Diagramming*

Teaching "The Significance of Film Form"

The Purpose of the Chapter

In some ways, this is the most important chapter in Film Art. It is designed to get students actively thinking about films as made up of many parts that relate dynamically to each other to make up a system. It suggests that they can and should participate actively in the viewing of any film, looking for individual devices and trying to explain why they are in the film and what effect they have on the viewer. In other words, Chapter Three suggests why close analysis of films is important.

The concept of the film's form as a system is

introduced early in the chapter. We stress that films are not random collections of technical devices. This picks up on Chapter One's emphasis on films as made objects. Similarly, it establishes Film Art's emphasis on looking at films as wholes. Most of the chapters will contain extended examples that examine film techniques in their contexts.

Much of the first half of Chapter Three is devoted to explaining how the spectator reacts actively to the film, forming expectations, drawing upon previous knowledge of conventions, reacting emotionally to what occurs on the screen, interpreting it, and evaluating the whole experience.

The second half of the chapter lays out the principles of film form. It also explains the concept of segmentation, or breaking a film down into parts for the purposes of analysis. All of these concepts will be crucial to the more specific subjects of later chapters.

Lecturing on and Discussing Film Form

Since it is vital that the students understand the basic concepts in this chapter, it might be valuable simply to go over these in class, giving additional examples. You might wish to illustrate your lecture with a short film containing a very obvious formal structure. Some possibilities would be Hilary Harris's Nine Variations on a Dance Theme, which presents the same dance filmed in nine successively more distorting styles, Robert Clampett's cartoon, Corny Concerto, with its three-short segments parodying Fantasia, and Robert Enrico's Occurrence at Owl Creek Bridge, which contains a frame story and flashback.

We have included extensive examples from a film which is probably familiar to virtually every student: The Wizard of Oz. This gives you the option of showing this or another film in your screening for this week. (It is best to stick to a fairly simple, straightforward film at this stage; see suggested titles at the end of this section.) Remind the students to take notes as they watch the film, recording their expectations and how they are fulfilled or thwarted, as well as other reactions they have as they watch the film and what triggered them. In discussion, you can go through the categories of film form as outlined in the chapter, asking your students to come up with examples of each type, to make sure that they understand each characteristic of film form. You should encourage them to ask questions during this discussion, since the concepts introduced in this chapter are more abstract than in any other part of Film Art.

Paper Topics on Segmentation

It is important for students to learn as soon as possible how to notice the large-scale parts of films. There are at least two ways of doing this, and you can choose to assign one or both. First, you can ask them to take notes on when scenes in the film you show that week begin and end. Then, in discussion, draw a horizontal line on the blackboard and make marks along it to indicate scenes, labelling each. Not every student will be able to keep track of every scene upon a single viewing, but among them they usually can come up with a good basic segmentation. (They must, however, be told in advance that this exercise will be part of the discussion.) For this purpose, it is a good idea to choose a film with a relatively small number of lengthy scenes (e.g., His Girl Friday) rather than one with many short scenes (e.g., Do The Right Thing).

A second approach to teaching segmentation would be a written assignment in which the student uses a video copy of a film and does a more formal, detailed segmentation of his or her own. This could be more or less elaborate. You could simply ask for a list of scenes, or ask the students in addition to explain what cues in the film led them to make the breaks where they did. Either of these segmentation exercises gives them an experience of doing basic analysis and prepares them for more complex work to come. As we shall see, they can be asked to do a more formal outline segmentation in connection with Chapter Four, on narrative form. Similarly, they can also be asked to do a more localized segmentation of a short scene in the form of a shot breakdown when you teach Chapter Eight, on film editing.

SUGGESTED FILMS

Primary example from chapter: The Wizard of Oz

Alternative films: *The Three Ages (Buster Keaton and Eddie Cline), North by Northwest (Alfred Hitchcock), Raging Bull (Martin Scorsese), *La Ronde (Max Ophuls), *Destiny (Fritz Lang), Stagecoach (John Ford; the first through fourth editions of Film Art contain an analysis of Stagecoach that might be of help in preparing a lecture on and/or discussion of this film), Jules and Jim (François Truffaut), Picnic at Hanging Rock (Peter Weir), Hannah and Her Sisters (Woody Allen; again, the first through fourth editions of Film Art contain an analysis of this film that you might wish to draw upon).

(Note: Films marked with an * contain a series of stories with particularly apparent similarities and differences among them.)

EXAMINATION QUESTIONS

Because Chapter Three deals with abstract concepts, it is very difficult to test using short objective questions. We suggest using essay-based examinations. The following questions could be adapted for a take-home exam or a paper assignment by deemphasizing the definition portions of the question and stressing the examples. You might assign the students to see a film on their own, either in a theater or on video, and draw upon it for examples that illustrate the concepts in Chapter Three.

Essay Questions

Drawing your examples from the opening sequences of [title of film shown in class], write a brief essay describing how this sequence generates expectations about the film's development. Use concrete examples to illustrate your points.

Distinguish between interpretation and evaluation of a film. What are some typical interpretive remarks that a critic might use in discussing [title of film shown in class]? What are some evaluative claims that a critic might make about it? Cite specific aspects of the film that might be used as evidence for each.

Describe the differences between the four kinds of meaning, referential, explicit, implicit, and symptomatic, using examples from The Wizard of Oz or [title of film shown in class].

Evaluation of films is done on the basis of objective criteria. What are some of these criteria and how could they be applied in evaluating [title of film or films shown in class]? [Or you might ask the students to use the criteria to evaluate a film of their choice which they have seen recently.]

Define "function" and "motivation" as they apply to film form, giving specific examples from Film Art, the lecture, or [title of film shown in class].

Define "motif" as it applies to film form, giving specific examples from Film Art, the lecture, or [title of film shown in class].

Explain three specific factors that help create unity in a film? Give some specific examples, drawing on Film Art, the lecture, or [title of film shown in class].

CHAPTER FOUR

NARRATIVE AS A FORMAL SYSTEM

Chapter Outline

Principles of Narrative Construction
Plot and Story
Cause and Effect
Time
*Openings, Closings, and Patterns of
    Development*
Narration: The Flow of Story Information
Range of Story Information
Depth of Story Information
The Narrator
The Classical Hollywood Cinema
Narrative Form in *Citizen Kane*
Overall Narrative Expectations
Plot and Story in ***Citizen Kane***
Citizen Kane's *Causality*
Time
Motivation
Parallelism
Patterns of Plot Development
Narration in ***Citizen Kane***
Notes and Queries
Narrative Form
The Spectator
Narrative Time
Narration
Narrative Analyses of Films
"Rosebud"

Teaching "Narrative as a Formal System"

The Purpose of the Chapter

<u>Film Art</u> distinguishes among five general
types of form: narrative, categorical, rhetorical, abstract, and associational. Because narrative form is the most familiar type and because so
many of the films we ordinarily see involve narra-

tives, we begin with that type and devote an entire chapter to it.

Because narrative form is so familiar, we seldom stop to think about what a narrative consists of and how it affects us. This chapter aims to get students to step back and examine aspects of storytelling that they usually take for granted. They should come to realize that viewing a narrative film is not simply a passive activity and that they as viewers are actively engaged in forming expectations about what will happen and in keeping track of how events relate to each other.

One basic tool for the students' examination of narrative form is the distinction between plot (the events as they are presented on the screen) and story (the events as we mentally reconstruct them in chronological order). Understanding the plot-story distinction will help the students think of narrative films as constructed by filmmakers. Moreover, the construction of the story (e.g., figuring out how events depicted in flashbacks fit into the story's chronology) is one of the activities that makes us participate in the ongoing development of the film.

Causal, spatial, and temporal relations among events are the building blocks of a film's narrative. They provide the student with the basic tools to discover how we can understand narratives. Causal and temporal factors, for example, are what enables us to understand the very concept of a flashback, as well as to figure out when its events occurred in relation to the rest of the action.

Finally, the concept of narration, the range and depth of which varies enormously from film to film, sheds light on the process by which narratives convey information to the spectator. Armed with this small number of important concepts, your students should be able to carry out narrative analysis.

Lecturing On and Discussing Narrative Form

The main example of a narrative film used in Chapter Four is <u>Citizen Kane</u>. This is the most important example used in the entire textbook, and it is dealt with extensively here and again in Chapter Ten, "Style as a Formal System." Teachers use Citizen Kane in their introductory courses more frequently than any other film. It offers an ideal example of narrative form, since its complex flashback structure shows the students quite clearly how the order of events as presented in the film's plot can differ greatly from the way we as spectators sort out those events as we reconstruct the story mentally.

Citizen Kane also offers the benefit of using all four areas of filmic technique flamboyantly, so that you can use examples from it in teaching Chapters Six through Nine; ideally it could be shown a second time, in conjunction with either one of those chapters or Chapter Ten.

If you decide to show a film other than Citizen Kane, it would be best to choose one with at least one flashback. Mystery films are also helpful, since there is usually a scene near the end when many earlier events are revealed for the first time.

Even though the plot-story distinction is basically a simple concept, students sometimes find it difficult to grasp at first. You might wish to go over the distinction in your lecture before the students see the film, then go over it in discussion until you are sure they understand it. You might also consider showing a short film with a simple scrambling of temporal order (e.g., Robert Clampett's The Old Grey Hare which flashes back to Bugs Bunny's and Elmer's Fudd's childhood) and make an outline of it. If you show Citizen Kane, you might go over the subsection on "Time" in the section "Narrative Form in Citizen Kane" and expand on our little outline of "Boyhood" to "Old age" by asking the students to recall other events associated with those sections and when we learn about them.

Similar tactics can be used to teach the somewhat difficult concepts of narrational range and depth. If you show Citizen Kane, try going through the subsection, "Narration in Citizen Kane" in some detail during discussion. One topic could be to tease out additional effects of the narration's refusal to allow us access to the minds of Mrs. Kane and Charles Foster Kane.

If you have time to show a second film and you wish to present a particular challenge, you might show one of these films (or others like them): Meshes of the Afternoon (Maya Deren), Un chien andalou (Luis Buñuel), The End (Christopher Maclaine), Entr'acte (René Clair), Refections on Black (Stan Brakhage), as these are all experimental films that take a very different approach to narrative. Another possibility is to show a film in which it is impossible to reconstruct a coherent story, due to contradictions or enigmas in the plot. Such films are rare but intriguing; a few examples: Last Year at Marienbad (Alain Resnais), Rashomon (Akira Kurosawa), and 12 Monkeys (Terry Gilliam).

Assigning a Paper on Narrative Form

A basic paper assignment would be to have your students make a segmentation of a film's narrative, using as a model the segmentation that appears early in the section, "Narrative Form in Citizen Kane. (This should work even if you show them another film in place of Citizen Kane.) Ideally they would need some way to see their film on video, as making a segmentation (particularly of a complex film) sometimes depends on being able to stop the film. But with a fairly straightforward narrative film, they may be able to do a segmentation as they watch a film in projection.

You may wish to prepare for this assignment by segmenting a short film or a portion of a feature along with the students, either in lecture or during discussion.

For a longer and more complex paper, you could assign your students to write a narrative analysis of a film, applying one or all of the main concepts discussed in Chapter Four, depending upon the length of the paper.

SUGGESTED FILMS

Primary example from chapter: Citizen Kane

Alternative films: Hiroshima mon amour (Alain

Resnais), <u>Double Indemnity</u> (Billy Wilder), <u>The Ceremony</u> (Nagisa Oshima), <u>8 1/2</u> (Federico Fellini), <u>Anatomy of a Murder</u> (Otto Preminger), <u>How Green Was My Valley</u> (John Ford), <u>Love Affair, or The Case of the Missing Switchboard Operator</u> (Dusan Makaveyev), <u>Stage Fright</u> (Alfred Hitchcock), <u>Laura</u> (Otto Preminger), <u>Le Jour se lève</u> (Marcel Carné)

EXAMINATION QUESTIONS

> in the margin indicates a question suitable for use in either a pop quiz or an exam.

Multiple-choice Questions

> In a narrative film, an element is nondiegetic if:

    a.   It does not contribute to the cause-effect flow of the events.

    b.   It is offscreen rather than onscreen.

*   c.   It is not part of the world of the depicted narrative.

    d.   It is not directly presented in the plot but can be inferred.

The opening scene of <u>Pulp Fiction</u> is an example of:

    a.   Expansion of temporal duration.

*   b.   A manipulation of temporal order.

    c.   An imbedded narrative.

    ·d.   Unrestricted narration.

"Depth" of narration refers to:

    a.   How quickly story information is provided to the audience.

    b.   How many lines of action the plot weaves

together.

c. How much information is presented by a nondiegetic narrator.

* d. How much the spectator learns about the characters' psychological states.

Which of the following statements is <u>not</u> true of the narration of George Miller's <u>The Road Warrior</u>?

a. The narration is mainly restricted to the hero Max's range of knowledge.

b. The narration provides shots from Max's optical point-of-view, as well as mental subjectivity.

* c. The mysterious narrator's voice from the opening scene turns out to be that of Max as an old man.

d. The narration withholds information so as to create a surprise ending.

> The chains of actions that make up the narratives of classical Hollywood films most typically depend upon:

* a. Psychological causes.

b. Social causes.

c. Natural causes.

d. Restricted causes.

Which of the following genres does <u>not</u> provide conventions used in <u>Citizen Kane</u>?

a. The musical

b. The detective story

c. The newspaper story

* d. The Western

> In <u>Citizen Kane</u>, the event that causes the report-
  er Thompson to write a story on Kane is:

      a.   Kane's second divorce.

      b.   Kane's inheritance of a mine.

*   c.   Kane's death.

      d.   Kane's first divorce.

The newsreel sequence in <u>Citizen Kane</u>:

      a.   Provides the only presentation of the
          events in Kane's life in chronological
          order.

*   b.   Presents a brief version of narrative
          events in roughly the same order as in
          the film as a whole.

      c.   Summarizes events we have already seen in
          flashback and provides a crucial clue to
          the narrative's resolution.

      d.   Finally gives the spectator an explana-
          tion of Kane's mysterious final word,
          "Rosebud."

> The ending of <u>Citizen Kane</u> is notable for:

*   a.   Its leaving the central mystery of the
          story partially open.

      b.   Its thorough resolution of an unusually
          large number of plot lines.

      c.   Its sudden introduction of a newsreel
          that summarizes and clarifies the narra-
          tive causality.

      d.   Its daring introduction of unmotivated
          causes that finally allow Thompson to
          achieve his goal.

<u>Film Art</u> argues that the search for the meaning of

"Rosebud" in <u>Citizen Kane</u> is more than a gimmick because:

  a. Thompson's discovery of "Rosebud" is what permits the narrative to achieve complete closure.

  b. The "Rosebud" motif creates parallelisms among all the flashbacks.

* c. The search provides a cause that motivates an investigation into character traits.

  d. "Rosebud" provides vital motivation about why Kane's mother sent him to live with Thatcher.

<u>Citizen Kane</u> creates a narrative parallel between Kane's political campaign and:

  a. His attempt to promote Bernstein despite Thatcher's objections.

  b. The montage sequence of Kane's first marriage deteriorating.

  c. His attempt to make Leland into a famous drama critic.

* d. His attempt to foster Susan's operatic career.

Which of the following statements is <u>not</u> true of the narration in <u>Citizen Kane</u>?

  a. The multiple flashbacks narrated by different characters yield restricted, generally objective information about Kane.

* b. For much of the film, the information presented by the narration is largely limited in range to the reporter Thompson's knowledge.

      c. At the beginning and ending of the film, the narration moves outside the range of knowledge of any of the characters.

      d. The flashbacks are used both to reveal and to conceal story information.

True-False Questions

> T̲ F Narrative form can be used in documentary films.

  T F̲ The opening scene of <u>North by Northwest</u> contains no nondiegetic elements.

  T̲ F Howard Hawks's <u>The Big Sleep</u> is an example of objective, highly restricted narration.

> T F̲ In a narrative film, plot duration is always equal to story duration.

  T F̲ Alfred Hitchcock's approach to narration is to withhold as much information as possible from the spectator in order to create surprise.

  T̲ F The plot duration of <u>Citizen Kane</u> consists of the time from Kane's death to the end of Thompson's investigation.

> T F̲ In <u>Citizen Kane</u>, the pattern of plot development is to move from flashbacks of Kane as an old man progressively back to flashbacks of him as a child.

Essay Questions

Explain the distinction made in <u>Film Art</u> between "plot" and "story" in narrative films. Use specific examples from <u>Film Art</u>, the lecture, and [title of film shown in class].

Discuss some of the ways in which a spectator actively participates in understanding the narrative of a film. Give specific examples from <u>Film Art</u>, the lecture, and any of the narrative films shown for this course.

Explain why it is often useful to compare the opening and closing of a film in analyzing its narrative. Give some specific examples from Film Art, the lecture, and any of the narrative films shown for this course.

Explain the term "narration," making reference in the course of your discussion to the concepts of range and depth. Use specific examples from Film Art, the lecture, and any of the narrative films shown for this course.

Discuss how causality operates in two or three scenes from [title of film shown in class]. Be sure to describe how specific events motivate other events.

Define the terms "order," "duration," and "frequency" as they apply to narrative time. Give specific examples of each from Film Art, the lecture, and any of the narrative films shown for this course.

Describe at least two basic narrative traits of the classical Hollywood cinema and give examples of each from Film Art, the lecture, and films shown in class.

[The following question can be used if you show your class a film that presents a distinct alternative to the classical Hollywood cinema] Describe two significant ways in which the narrative of [film title] departs from the classical Hollywood cinema's tradition. Be as specific as possible in giving examples from the film.

Discuss at least two ways in which Citizen Kane's narrative adheres to conventions of classical Hollywood narrative and some of the ways in which it departs from that tradition.

Discuss at least two ways in which Citizen Kane's plot differs from its underlying story. Be as specific as you can in giving examples of manipulations of temporal order, duration, and frequency.

Explain how <u>Citizen Kane</u>'s narrative fails to achieve complete closure and discuss some of the effects this has on the spectator's understanding of the film.

CHAPTER FIVE

NONNARRATIVE FORMAL SYSTEMS

Chapter Outline

Teaching "Nonnarrative Formal Systems"

The Purpose of the Chapter

Most students will have had some experience
in watching a variety of films containing all four
types of nonnarrative form we discuss in Chapter
Five--if mainly on television. Many advertise-
ments and TV "magazine" shows use rhetorical form,
while music videos frequently develop through
associations rather than narrative.

As in dealing with narrative form, our purpose is to make students aware of types of filmic
experiences that they ordinarily take for granted.
Categorical, rhetorical, abstract, and associational form are not intended as dry categories
into which we sort films, but as ways of describing how different types of form have profound

effects on the way spectators perceive films.

At the least, after reading this chapter and seeing some pertinent examples, students should be aware of the wide variety of films there are in the world. Beyond this, some of them may be intrigued and continue after the course ends to seek out films that use all kinds of formal possibilities.

Teaching Nonnarrative Form

Years ago, when we added a chapter on this subject to Film Art, there was no useful classification of nonnarrative films. We devised four types, and we believe that virtually all nonnarrative films fall into them. Even though many films mix types (combining, say, a rhetorical argument with a set of categories), in most cases one type of nonnarrative form can be determined to be the one that dominates and has the most control over the film's overall form.

Still, because we have devised these distinctions among types of nonnarrative form, they will be new to students, who will need help in mastering them conceptually. One way to approach this chapter is to show several short films that are distinct examples of each type of form (with little mixing of types, at least to begin with). It would be possible, for example, to show Olympia, Part 2 as the main film for the week, then during the lecture to show some short films that illustrate the three other types of form. For example, you might show Shirley Clarke's Bridges Go Round. It is only three-and-a-half minutes long, yet it gives a very clear demonstration of abstract form. Although the whole film consists of images of bridges, Clarke was obviously more interested in shapes, patterns, movements, and color than in the category of "bridges" as such.

Another possibility might be to show Housing Problems (1936), the classic British documentary that pioneered the interview technique that has become such a crucial part of both film and television documentaries. Made by a British gas company, it argues for modernization by the installation of natural gas in homes. The bulk of the film consists of interviews with working-class people living in poor conditions, without gas, and ends with those in better circumstances who have natural gas. This film could be paired with Nick Parks's animated short, Creature Comforts (a five-minute gem that proves categorical form is not just used in documentaries), which is a parody of Housing Problems and similar "talking heads" films. Creature Comforts uses claymation techniques to create "interview" with zoo animals, some of whom have complaints about their quarters and others who do not (but probably should). Although Creature Comforts implies a problem with typical zoo policies (cramped quarters), it sets forth no argument about how that problem might be solved. It remains an example of categorical form, organized around interviews with a variety of zoo inhabitants.

Alternatively, you might wish to create a program for your weekly screening, showing only a portion of Olympia, Part 2 and combining it with the other films discussed in the chapter to make your full weekly program. (Again, it would be a good idea to show a few additional short examples during lecture or discussion.) If you take this approach, it would be better not to show the diving sequence as your sole excerpt, since it could mislead the students into thinking that this film is organized around abstract form. The early sequences or the cross-country riding and crew sections would be more indicative of the film's categorical form.

Once you have given several clear examples of the four types of nonnarrative form, you might wish to include an example or two of films that mix types. A brief film of this type could, for example, be shown late in a discussion session, leading to an exchange among the students as to which type of form ultimately is dominant.

Assigning a Paper on Nonnarrative Form

You may find it useful to assign a short paper on nonnarrative form. This can be done by showing some additional films in class or making a variety of films available to the students on

47

video tape. Many video stores also classify their films so as to have sections on experimental and documentary films, so you may want them to track down nonnarrative films on their own. (Note, however, that many experimental and documentary films use narrative form, so you may need to give the students guidance and suggestions to help them find appropriate subjects for their papers.) The assignment would be to describe the film, classifying it into one of the four types of nonnarrative form and explaining why it falls into that classification by citing evidence from the film.

SUGGESTED FILMS

Primary examples from chapter: Olympia, Pt. 2 (categorical form), The River (rhetorical form), Ballet mécanique (abstract form), A Movie (associational form)

Alternative films:

Categorical Form: Every Day Except Christmas (Lindsay Anderson), Thursday's Children (Lindsay Anderson), Let There Be Light (John Huston), Wild Wheels (Harrod Blank), films by Frederick Wiseman (e.g., Law and Order, Hospital), Zorns Lemma (Hollis Frampton), Creature Comforts (Nick Park)

Abstract Form: Bridges Go Round (Shirley Clarke), Motion Painting #1 (Oskar Fischinger), Nine Variations on a Dance Theme (Hilary Harris), Fist Fight (Robert Breer), A Study in Choreography for the Camera (Maya Deren), Dom (Jan Lenica and Walerian Browczyk), Critical Mass (Hollis Frampton)

Rhetorical Form: The Plow That Broke the Plains (Pare Lorentz), Harvest of Shame (David Lowe), Smoke Menace (John Taylor), Housing Problems (Edgar Anstey and Arthur Elton), London Can Take It (Harry Watt and Humphrey Jennings), The Spanish Earth (Joris Ivens), Prelude to War (Frank Capra)

Associational Form: Cosmic Ray (Bruce Conner), Report (Bruce Conner), To Parsifal (Bruce Baillie), Mass for the Dakota Sioux (Bruce Baillie),

Song of Ceylon (Basil Wright), Koyaanisqatsi (Godfrey Reggio), Powaqqatsi (Godfrey Reggio), L'Étoile de mer (Man Ray), Scorpio Rising (Kenneth Anger), Breathdeath (Stan Van Der Beek), Rose Hobart (Joseph Cornell), Unsere Afrikareise (Peter Kubelka), A propos de Nice (Jean Vigo)

EXAMINATION QUESTIONS

> in the margin indicates a question suitable for use in either a pop quiz or an exam.

Multiple-choice Questions

> Which of the following is not a typical strategy of categorical form used in Harrod Blank's Wild Wheels?

*   a.   It creates a rigorously logical set of categories of decorated cars.

       b.   It follows a simple pattern of development.

       c.   It occasionally introduces scenes organized around formal systems other than categorical.

       d.   It creates transitions by finding overlaps among its categories.

> Leni Riefenstahl's Olympia, Part 2 is an example of:

       a.   Rhetorical form.

       b.   Abstract form.

*   c.   Categorical form.

       d.   Associational form.

The opening of Leni Riefenstahl's Olympia, Part 2:

       a.   Emphasizes the many different nationalities of the spectators crowding into the

Olympic stadium.

* b. Initially plays down the nationalities of the contestants, emphasizing camaraderie.

   c. Creates a prologue by showing Adolf Hitler's plane descending majestically through the clouds as he travels to attend the games.

   d. Draws upon abstract form to create a dynamic sequence of divers seen against the sky.

The use of Nazi ideology in Leni Riefenstahl's Olympia, Part 2 could best be described as:

   a. An explicit motif that Riefenstahl frequently emphasizes.

   b. Entirely suppressed in order to sell the film abroad.

* c. An occasional motif that creates an implicit meaning.

   d. Displayed according to which games and athletes the director chose to include.

> Which of the following types of argument is not typical of rhetorical form?

   a. Arguments from source

   b. Subject-centered arguments

   c. Viewer-centered arguments

* d. Arguments from effect

> Pare Lorentz's The River bases its rhetorical argument on:

   a. Contrasting interviews with both politicians and ordinary inhabitants of the Tennessee Valley.

b. Interviews with scientists who offer expert opinions on dam-building and flooding.

* c. An historical description of erosion along the Mississippi and rivers that flow into it.

d. Intercutting scenes of flooding in the Midwest with excerpts from a speech by Franklin Roosevelt describing the benefits of the Tennessee Valley Authority.

Which of the following is not a rhetorical strategy used in Pare Lorentz's The River?

a. A voice-over narrator with an authoritative voice

b. A poetically repetitious voice-over narration

* c. A motif of cheerful workers on Tennessee Authority Valley dams

d. Shots stressing the ecological destruction of timberland in the Midwest

When Pare Lorentz's The River was released in the late 1930s:

a. It was seen only in a few theaters, due to exhibitors' reluctance to show such a long documentary on their programs.

b. It impressed Pentagon officials so much that they later assigned Lorentz to direct the war-time documentary series "Why We Fight."

* c. It impressed President Roosevelt so much that he started the U. S. Film Service.

d. It became the first government-sponsored film to win an Oscar as best short documentary.

Film Art describes a common way of organizing films with abstract form as:

    a. A "graphic chain" of progression.

*   b. "Theme and variations."

    c. Visual "poetic" rhythm.

    d. Systematic balance versus imbalance.

> The "dance" in Léger and Murphy's *Ballet mécanique* consists of:

    a. Hundreds of close, rhythmic shots of parts of a speeding locomotive.

    b. Modern dancers in shiny costumes moving with stiff, robot-like gestures.

    c. A variety of small, metallic objects that move in patterns created by the pixillation technique of animation.

*   d. A rhythmic juxtaposition of various ordinary objects, people, and writing.

True-False Questions

> T F   Riefenstahl's *Olympia*, Part 2 follows an ABA pattern of development.

   T F   Pare Lorentz's *The River* uses no music after the credits sequence ends in order to create an objective tone.

   T F   Pare Lorentz's *The River* compares three solutions to the problem of flooding before opting for one as the best.

> T F   It is possible to do segmentations of a film with narrative, categorical, rhetorical, or associational form but not of a film with abstract form.

> <u>T</u> F   Léger and Murphy's <u>Ballet mécanique</u> uses a
        theme and variations pattern of formal pro-
        gression.

Essay Questions

Briefly define the characteristics of categorical,
rhetorical, abstract, and associational formal
systems, giving specific examples from <u>Film Art</u>,
from lectures, and from films shown for the
course.

How may we distinguish a film using categorical
form from one using abstract form? Draw specific
examples from <u>Film Art</u>, from lectures, or from
films shown for the course.

How may we distinguish a film using rhetorical
form from one using associational form?   Draw
specific examples from <u>Film Art</u>, from lectures, or
from films shown for the course.

Some nonnarrative films draw on aspects of narrative form to organize sections or parts. Choose
one nonnarrative film which draws upon narrative
principles. What sort of nonnarrative principles
organize the overall film? How does it draw upon
narrative principles of organization? What purposes are fulfilled by the narrative portions of
the film?   Point to specific sequences which
support your claims.

CHAPTER SIX

THE SHOT: MISE-EN-SCENE

Chapter Outline

What is Mise-en-Scene?
Realism
The Power of Mise-en-Scene
Aspects of Mise-en-Scene
 Setting
 Costume and Make-up
 Lighting
 Figure Expression and Movement
Mise-en-Scene in Space and Time
 Space
 Time
Narrative Functions of Mise-en-Scene: *Our*
Hospitality
Summary

Notes and Queries
 On the Origins of Mise-en-Scene
 On Realism in Mise-en-Scene
 Computer Imaging and Mise-en-Scene
 Particular Aspects of Mise-en-Scene
 Depth
 Color Design
 Frame Composition and the Viewer's Eye

Teaching "The Shot: Mise-en-Scene"

The Purpose of the Chapter

Chapter Six is the first of four chapters devoted to the basic stylistic techniques of the cinema: mise-en-scene, cinematography, editing, and sound. We have chosen this order because it leads the student through increasing levels of difficulty. We begin with mise-en-scene because it involves the persons, places, and things readily apparent on the screen.

This chapter aims to get students thinking analytically about matters which they are accus-

tomed to noticing casually in their ordinary film-
going: acting, set design, lighting, make-up, and
staging of movement. They should come to realize
that all the elements placed before the camera
result from a complex series of decisions by the
filmmakers and have an enormous impact on the
spectator.

Teaching Mise-en-scene

Chapter Six is a particularly important one
for broadening students' range of experience in
films. We have mentioned that students often come
into introductory courses unaccustomed to watching
older films and foreign films. Usually their
resistance is based on filmic elements that fall
into the category of mise-en-scene. Older styles
of acting are particularly hard for them to adjust
to, and they may dismiss some films as not looking
realistic. Thus the short but important section
on realism could be stressed. In lecture you
could give additional examples, both of films that
deliberately avoid realism and of those that have
been considered realistic in the past. Similarly,
in discussion you might elicit examples of the
same kinds of films from the students themselves.
Similar tactics can help them get used to watching
a greater variety of acting styles than they are
used to.

You might also consider showing the students
all or part of the videotape Michael Caine on
Acting in Film; it vividly demonstrates that an
actor's performance can result from careful crafting in much the way that a set is designed or a
dance choreographed. It also illustrates the
point made in Film Art, that camera distance is a
crucial factor for an actor crafting his/her
performance. It also touches on material from
other chapters, discussing the "master shot" and
closer shots (introduced in Chapter One) and
continuity, especially as it relates to matching
actors' gestures (see Chapter Eight). (You should
be able to order this videotape through a local
video store; it is also available from Applause
Theater Books, 211 West 71st Street, New York NY
10023. A book based on the video, Acting in Film:

An Actor's Take on Movie Making, was also issued by Applause in 1990.)

Lighting is the most difficult mise-en-scene technique for most students to notice on the screen. They may also have difficulty grasping how lights are set up in a film studio. *Film Art*'s overhead diagram of three-point lighting lays out the basic system, but it is necessarily limited by being two-dimensional. If you have a relatively small class, you might consider doing a brief demonstration during lecture, darkening the room and setting ordinary lamps in various positions around an object or person to show the wide variety of possible effects (e.g., placing a single bright lamp behind the subject should give a vivid instance of backlighting).

In the suggestions for Chapter Seven, on cinematography, we discuss the possibility of showing the documentary <u>Visions of Light: The Art of Cinematography</u>. You might want to show it during your unit on mise-en-scene instead, since, as its title suggests, it deals very extensively with lighting. It would also then prepare the students for the next chapter.

Assigning a Paper on Mise-en-Scene

A simple assignment for a short paper would be to have the student watch a film (preferably twice), choosing one or more motifs of mise-en-scene, and listing them, noting how each functions in the context of the film's form. Motifs like props and costumes are relatively easy to notice and hence the students will probably choose in those categories. If you wish to challenge them more, specify that they look for motifs of lighting as well.

For a longer paper, you could simply expand this assignment and have your students write on all aspects of mise-en-scene in a single film.

SUGGESTED FILMS

Primary example from chapter: <u>Our Hospitality</u>

Alternative films: <u>The General</u> (Buster Keaton),

Foolish Wives (Erich von Stroheim), Ivan the Terrible (Sergei Eisenstein), Trouble in Paradise (Ernst Lubitsch), Rebecca (Alfred Hitchcock), The Band Wagon (Vincente Minelli), Play Time (Jacques Tati), Shanghai Express (Josef von Sternberg), Paris, Texas (Wim Wenders), Brazil (Terry Gilliam)

EXAMINATION QUESTIONS

> in the margin indicates a question suitable for use in either a pop quiz or an exam.

Multiple-choice Questions

> Which of the following is not considered part of a shot's mise-en-scene:

    a.   The actors' movements.

*   b.   The camera's angle on the action.

    c.   Objects visible in the distance.

    d.   The shadows.

A major example of highly distorted set design is:

    a.   Greed.

    b.   Intolerance.

    c.   The Outlaw and His Wife.

*   d.   The Cabinet of Dr. Caligari.

The system of lighting widely used in classical Hollywood filmmaking is known as:

*   a.   Three-point lighting.

    b.   Five-point lighting.

    c.   Cast-shadow lighting.

    d.   Omnidirectional lighting.

Which of the following is <u>not</u> a term for a type of directional lighting?

    a. Toplighting

    b. Underlighting

*   c. Overlighting

    d. Backlighting

> According to <u>Film Art</u>, film actor's performance style is most affected by:

    a. The microphone placement.

*   b. The camera distance.

    c. The aspect ratio.

    d. The lighting.

"Frontality" of staging means that:

    a. A character is placed in the extreme foreground of the shot.

*   b. A character is facing toward the camera.

    c. One character blocks our view of another.

    d. A character is moving toward the foreground.

Which of the following is <u>not</u> a motif in the mise-en-scene in Buster Keaton's <u>Our Hospitality</u>?

    a. A sampler embroidered "Love Thy Neighbor"

    b. A fish-on-a-line motif

    c. A gun rack

*   d. A dog-on-a-leash motif

> Georges Méliès was:

* a. An early director of fantasy films.

    b. An important French set designer of the 1930s.

    c. The director of <u>Our Hospitality</u>.

    d. The first historian to study mise-en-scene.

"Stop-action" involves:

    a. Having actors stand in the same spot where they were at the end of one shot while the lighting is adjusted for the next shot.

    b. Halting the filming in one set and moving on to another while shooting out of continuity.

    c. One actor in a scene refrain from any obvious movement after delivering a line so as not to call attention away from the actor who is responding.

* d. Animating an object by changing its position between each frame shot.

Aerial perspective suggests depth by:

* a. Making more distant planes seem hazier than closer ones.

    b. Creating a high angle that makes parallel lines meet at the horizon.

    c. Composing a shot that makes the sky dominate the image.

    d. Filming from directly above down on a character or setting.

Perspective diminution suggests depth by:

a. Making parallel lines seem to intersect.

b. Creating false perspective by placing taller characters closer to the camera and shorter characters farther off.

* c. Implying that the elements which are smaller in the shot tend to be farther away.

d. Reduces the cues for perspective so that the space appears relatively shallow.

True-false Questions

> T <u>F</u> The two basic types of light in a scene are the key and the rim.

> <u>T</u> F Animated films, like live-action films, have mise-en-scene.

T <u>F</u> Unplanned events that are filmed by accident are not part of the mise-en-scene of a shot.

<u>T</u> F Marlon Brando's performance in <u>On the Waterfront</u> was a major example of realistic acting.

T <u>F</u> Films shot in the studio have mise-en-scene, while films made entirely on location do not.

T <u>F</u> "Fill" light is used to create deep shadows.

<u>T</u> F "Edge" lighting is a type of backlighting used to make characters stand out against a background.

> T <u>F</u> In Hollywood studio filmmaking, the lights are kept in the same position throughout a scene, no matter where the camera is placed.

> <u>T</u> F "High-key" lighting is typical of Hollywood filmmaking.

T <u>F</u> Soft, high-key lighting is associated with mystery stories, crime films, and <u>films</u>

<u>noirs</u>.

> T <u>F</u> According to <u>Film Art</u>, realism is the most useful standard for evaluating actors' performances.

  T <u>F</u> German Expressionist films like <u>The Cabinet of Dr. Caligari</u> are characterized by realistic mise-en-scene and subtle, psychologically based acting.

  <u>T</u> F "Warm" colors tend to attract the spectator's eye more than "cool" colors do.

  T <u>F</u> To achieve variety and visual interest, most directors try to keep the compositions of their shots unbalanced.

Essay Questions

Discuss the problems with using realism as a criterion for evaluating films, giving specific examples from any of the films shown for this class.

[Leave a slide that exemplifies all four aspects of mise-en-scene on the screen for the duration of this question or show a brief clip a few times] Describe and discuss the functions of the mise-en-scene in this shot/these shots. Mention at least one example of each of the four major categories of mise-en-scene.

[Show a brief clip from a film, preferably one the students have seen before; if the film is in black and white, substitute "tonality" or "lighting" for "color" in the question.] Discuss which compositional elements (moving objects versus static ones, color, balance, and size) guide our eye around the screen in the shots in the clip. Be as specific as possible in your descriptions.

[Show a slide or a brief clip from a film, preferably one the students have seen.] Discuss which depth cues (overlap, aerial perspective, size

diminution) are used to create an illusion of three-dimensional space in these shots.
[Note: To make this question more challenging, eliminate "(overlap, aerial perspective, size diminution)".]

[These two questions could be used together with the same clip; show the clip a second time halfway through the time allotted for the questions. For more challenging questions, ask the students to name the compositional and depth cues in each question. Note that since movement is an important cue both for compositional attention and depth, these two questions work best with a clip, though they could be used with a slide.]

CHAPTER SEVEN

THE SHOT: CINEMATOGRAPHY

Chapter Outline

> **The Photographic Image**
> > *The Range of Tonalities*
> > *Speed of Motion*
> > *Perspective Relations*
>
> **Framing**
> > *Frame Dimensions and Shape*
> > *Onscreen and Offscreen Space*
> > *Angle, Level, Height, and Distance of*
> > > *Framing*
> > *The Mobile Frame*
>
> **Duration of the Image: The Long Take**
> > *The Long Take*
>
> **Notes and Queries**
> > *General Works*
> > *Color versus Black and White*
> > *Perspective and the Cinema*
> > *Special Effects*
> > *Aspect Ratio*
> > *The Subjective Shot*
> > *Camera Movement and Zoom*
> > *"Real Time" and the Long Take*

Teaching "The Shot: Cinematography"

<u>The Purpose of the Chapter</u>

Aside from the Sample Analyses (Chapter Eleven), this is the longest chapter in <u>Film Art</u>. This is because cinematography is such a complex subject. The modern motion-picture camera and raw stock offer an enormous range of technical possibilities for lens length, shooting speed, aspect ratio, color, and camera movement--all of which profoundly affect the look of the film. Moreover the filmmakers make a huge number of aesthetic decisions about how to frame their images.

Chapter Seven aims to introduce students to

all the basic possibilities of cinematography, with an emphasis on what the various techniques and framing choices look like on the screen. Hence this is the most heavily illustrated chapter in the book, with well over two hundred frame enlargements.

Here for the first time the students are being asked to look not just at what they are seeing (actors wearing costumes, moving around sets, and so on) but how the film presents the mise-en-scene elements to them. By the end of this unit of the course, they should be able to look at films in a new way. They will have gained the vocabularly to describe all the visual elements of a shot. For example, they will know that the opening of Touch of Evil is not just a scene of a couple strolling across the Mexican border, unaware of a bomb in a car that passes them. They will be able to specify that it is a craning and tracking long take that begins on a close-up framing and ends on a medium-long framing.

Lecturing on and Discussing Cinematography

Though the look of a film depends fundamentally upon cinematography, students will initially have more trouble "seeing" cinematographic techniques than noticing aspects of mise-en-scene. It is quite easy to grasp the contrast in the two hats worn by Hildie in His Girl Friday (an example used in Chapter Six). It is less easy to distinguish a panning movement to the right from a tracking movement in the same direction.

Thus it is a good idea to use as many slides and clips as possible. Grasping cinematographic technique is largely a matter of practice. Part of the discussion session could be given over to watching a variety of clips, with the students identifying the devices used in each shot. Watching films with the sound turned off is helpful to prevent students from getting caught up in the action and forgetting to watch the cinematography. (If you have some students who find it particularly difficult to notice cinematographic techniques, suggest that they try this for themselves by watching a few films on video without the sound.)

64

You might also consider showing the ninety-minute documentary film, <u>Visions of Light: The Art of Cinematography</u> (1993, Arnold Glassman, Todd McCarthy, and Stuart Samuels). It contains excerpts from over eighty films (mostly sound and American, but with a sampling of silent and foreign films) and interviews with many cinematographers. While many of the clips are quite short, there can be few ways of exposing a beginning student to such a variety of styles in such a short time. Some of the commentary by the cinematographers is quite insightful, and there is documentary footage of cinematographers in action.

<u>Visions of Light</u> has the advantage of treating older films with extraordinary reverence, and it could convince students that there is something worth watching in the black-and-white classics they might otherwise resist. It also uses many of the terms introduced in <u>Film Art</u> (e.g., high-key light) and shows some of the shots illustrated in the text (e.g., the Steadicam view of Jake moving through the corridor and into the ring in <u>Raging Bull</u>). In general, the film contains clips from many films that are dealt with in <u>Film Art</u>, including <u>Citizen Kane</u>, <u>The Wizard of Oz</u>, <u>Meet Me in St. Louis</u>, <u>Touch of Evil</u>, <u>Raging Bull</u>, and <u>Do The Right Thing</u>. Finally, Vittorio Storaro (cinematographer of <u>Apocalypse Now</u> and <u>The Last Emperor</u>) reprises our discussion in Chapter One of why the director is usually considered the "author" of a film.

Assigning a Paper on Cinematography

The same basic topic described in the section on mise-en-scene in Chapter Six could be assigned, but with the students directed to write on one or more motifs of cinematography in a film.

SUGGESTED FILMS

Primary example from chapter: <u>Grand Illusion</u>

Alternative films: <u>The Rules of the Game</u> (Jean Renoir), <u>Ugetsu Monogatari</u> (Kenji Mizoguchi), <u>Sunrise</u> (F. W. Murnau), <u>Touch of Evil</u> (Orson

Welles), <u>For a Few Dollars More</u> (Sergio Leone), <u>Breathless</u> (Jean-Luc Godard), <u>Cronaca di un amore</u> (Michelangelo Antonioni), <u>Vampyr</u> (Carl Theodor Dreyer), <u>Metropolis</u> (Fritz Lang), <u>Lola Montès</u> (Max Ophuls), <u>The Long Goodbye</u> (Robert Altman), <u>The Untouchables</u> (Brian De Palma)

EXAMINATION QUESTIONS

> in the margin indicates a question suitable for use in either a pop quiz or an exam.

Multiple-choice Questions

Technicolor was notable for:

    a. Its soft, warm pastels.

    b. Its ease of use during shooting.

* c. Its rich, saturated hues.

    d. Requiring considerably less light than earlier color processes.

Tinting and toning are:

    a. Printing techniques used to correct flaws in an image's color.

    b. Make-up used to adjust skin tones to suit the color balance of the film stock.

    c. Two methods of using filters to change the color of the light on the set.

* d. Dyes used to add color to black-and-white film.

Standard projection speed for sound films is:

* a. 24 frames per second.

    b. 50 feet per minute.

    c. 36 frames per second.

d. 30 minutes per reel.

> Which of the following is <u>not</u> affected by the focal length of the camera lens?

    a. Magnification

    b. Depth

    c. Scale

*   d. Aspect ratio ·

A zoom lens is:

    a. A lens with an extremely long focal length.

*   b. A lens which can change focal length while a shot is being filmed.

    c. A lens with a special mount that can be changed very quickly between shots.

    d. A short lens used for rapid camera movements.

"Depth of field" refers to:

    a. The distance the actors have to be from the camera to prevent their heads from going out of the frame.

    b. The distance from the camera to the back wall of the set.

*   c. The range of distances from the lens in which objects filmed will be in focus.

    d. How large objects appear within the frame.

Deep-focus cinematography was popularized by:

    a. <u>Gone with the Wind</u>.

b. The Crime of M. Lange.

c. The Wizard of Oz.

*   d. Citizen Kane.

"Process shots" refers to:

*   a. A type of special effects.

b. Shots using zooms in or out.

c. Shots filmed in slow or fast motion.

d. Shots made using time-lapse filming.

Which of the following is not a type of composite filming?

a. Matte

b. Rear projection

*   c. Superimposition

d. Front projection

The figures 1.33:1, 2.35:1, and 1.66:1 are all examples of:

a. Lens-length ratios.

b. Film-gauge ratios.

c. Perspective ratios.

*   d. Aspect ratios.

> Which of the following describes a type of wide-screen image?

*   a. Hard matte

b. Composite image

c. Full-frame

        d.   Academy ratio

> An anamorphic lens:

        a.   Has a built-in filter that permits "day-
              for-night" shooting.

*   b.   Is used to squeeze a widescreen image
              onto a strip of film.

        c.   Is specifically designed for use on a
              Steadicam.

        d.   Gives greater depth of field than any
              other type of lens.

In cinematography, "mask" refers to:

*   a.   A technique used to change the shape of
              the frame.

        b.   A filter placed over the lens to change
              the color of the scene.

        c.   The case placed around the camera to
              muffle its noise for sound filming.

        d.   Shades used to keep sunlight from creat-
              ing lens flares.

> In a canted camera position, objects on the screen
  appear:

        a.   Upside down.

*   b.   Not to be level.

        c.   As seen from directly above.

        d.   As seen at ground level.

Terms for camera distance, such as "medium shot,"
are based on:

        a.   The actual distance of the characters
              from the camera.

       b.   The focal length of the lens being used.

*   c.   The size of the figures relative to the
            frame.

       d.   How high the actors' heads are in the
            frame.

> Which of the following is <u>not</u> a standard term for
  a type of mobile framing?

       a.   Tilt

       b.   Crane

       c.   Pan

*   d.   Glide

"Reframing" refers to:

       a.   Taking one lens off the camera and putt-
            ing on another with a different focal
            length.

       b.   Moving the camera forward after the
            master shot has been filmed, in order to
            get closer views.

*   c.   Short pans or tilts to keep the composi-
            tion balanced.

       d.   Inserting hard mattes into the camera to
            achieve widescreen aspect ratios.

A central characteristic of the cinematography in
Jean Renoir's <u>Grand Illusion</u> is:

       a.   Long takes with a nearly static camera
            and complex staging in depth.

*   b.   Frequent tracking shots that emphasize
            significant details in the mise-en-scene.

       c.   Innovative use of the zoom shot.

d.   Almost constant craning shots.

The form of Michael Snow's <u>Wavelength</u> is struc-
tured around which type of mobile framing?

    a.   Slow tracking shots through an abandoned
       loft

    b.   Rhythmic panning to catch the reactions
       of a crowd

    c.   A series of slow craning shots on a
       beach

*   d.   An irregular series of zoom-ins across a
       room

Which group of filmmakers is typically associated
with the long take?

*   a.   Orson Welles, Kenji Mizoguchi, Andy
       Warhol, and Miklós Jancsó

    b.   Howard Hawks, Buster Keaton, Robert
       Bresson, and Louis Lumière

    c.   Georges Méliès, Akira Kurosawa, Abel
       Gance, and Sergei Eisenstein

    d.   Erich von Stroheim, Samuel Fuller, Alain
       Resnais, and Richard Lester

True-False Questions

<u>T</u> F   A low-contrast image displays a wide range of
     grays.

>   T <u>F</u>   Modern films that look quite bright on a
     theater screen will tend to look darker on
     television.

>   <u>T</u> F   Slow motion is achieved by speeding up the
     rate of filming.

>   T <u>F</u>   Wide-angle lenses are also referred to as

71

"telephoto" lenses.

T F A long focal-length lens tends to squash the planes of action together, reducing depth cues.

> T F "Rack focus" refers to adjusting the camera to change the plane that is in focus.

T F The Lumière brothers' early camera was too bulky to take on location, leading them to shoot in a film studio.

> T F "Pan-and-scan" is a method for showing wide-screen films on television.

T F A zoom lens allows filmmakers to magnify or demagnify objects without changing perspective relationships in the shot.

> T F A "long take" is a shot taken with the camera at a considerable distance from the main subject of the shot.

Essay Questions

[Leave a slide that exemplifies several aspects of cinematography on the screen for the duration of this question or show a brief clip a few times]
(a) Describe and discuss at least three aspects of the cinematography in this shot/these shots as you can in the time allotted. Be sure to discuss both the framing and the photographic qualities of the image.
(b) How do the factors you isolate contribute to the meaings and effects of the shot?

[Show a brief clip that makes significant and varied use of offscreen space.] Discuss the use of offscreen space in this shot/these shots. Then go on to describe some ways filmmakers can use offscreen space, drawing upon examples from Film Art, the lectures, and any of the films seen in this class.

Describe what offscreen space is and some of the ways it can be used. Give some specific examples from <u>Film Art</u>, the lecture, and any film seen for this class.

CHAPTER EIGHT

THE RELATION OF SHOT TO SHOT: EDITING

Chapter Outline

Teaching "The Relation of Shot to Shot: Editing"

The Purpose of the Chapter

Editing is perhaps the most difficult of the four types of film technique for students to notice systematically. Viewers may be aware of transitions from shot to shot when these are particularly noticeable, as with a slow dissolve, or a rapid burst of short, disorienting shots, or a cut accompanied by a burst of loud noise. On the whole, however, students are looking at what is in the shots, not how the spatial, temporal, rhythmic, and graphic aspects of shots are affected by the way they are edited together.

Moreover, editing is more difficult to grasp than, say, techniques of cinematography. A camera movement occupies time, and the student can watch it unfold. But a cut is instantaneous, and once it occurs, it may not be easy for the student to remember what had preceded the shot now on the screen.

Yet editing has an enormous impact on how we respond to films, and with a bit of practice one can become aware of editing without losing any enjoyment in watching the actions taking place on the screen. Chapter Eight aims to "freeze" the editing and to lay shots out systematically on the page so that students may study the typical patterns and possibilities of editing.

Lecturing On and Discussing Editing

Your students may find learning to watch for editing a bit frustrating at first. As with the other film techniques, you can help by showing as many slides and clips as possible. One valuable exercise is to show a clip, then go through it by showing slides of the beginning and ending of each shot. Editing is one technique that really benefits from the use of two slide projectors, so that you can put the end of one shot side by side with the beginning of the shot that follows, much as we have done with many of the frame enlargements in Chapter Eight. (Some slide duplicators with zoom functions also allow you to photograph the last frame of one shot along with the first frame of the next, thereby enabling you to show the cut itself with a single slide. See the section in Part III on "Making Slides from Film and Video Images.") After going through the slides, you could then show the same clip. Ideally this should be done first in lecture, with you pointing out the various editing techniques used in the clips. Then another clip could be shown during discussion (possibly from the main film shown for the class that week); ask the students to describe the editing techniques they see in the clip.

Another possibility for discussion is to go

through the extended example from The Maltese Falcon given in Chapter Eight. Since continuity editing is designed to be smooth and unobtrusive, the students may have particular trouble spotting cuts with matches on action, shot/reverse shot, and other techniques of the classical Hollywood system. Showing this scene from The Maltese Falcon at the beginning and ending of this portion of the discussion would enhance the lesson.

In Chapter Eight we suggest to the students that they can practice watching for editing by playing a video with the sound off, tapping or clapping at each cut. The same exercise can be done in lecture or discussion.

Assigning a Paper on Editing

One simple and useful assignment is to use video clips of a single scene and ask the students to write up a shot breakdown, or découpage. The format for this could be modelled on the brief shot lists given for The Birds early in Chapter Eight. Have the students number the shots and use the standard abbreviations (LS, MS, CU, etc.) for each. They will not be able to give precise timings in number of frames, as we do, but you can ask them to give rough timings in seconds. They should specify the camera angle and any camera movement. They should also give brief descriptions of the action and suggest functions which the shot-changes serve.

Alternatively, you could set aside discussion time and do this shot breakdown by showing a clip several times and writing the students' verbal descriptions on the blackboard. Or you could begin with an in-class exercise of this type, then ask the students to do a written shot breakdown on their own, as described above.

For a longer, more challenging paper, the same basic topic described in the section on mise-en-scene in Chapter Six could be assigned, but with the students directed to write on one or more motifs of editing in a film.

76

SUGGESTED FILMS

Primary examples from chapter: <u>The Birds</u>, <u>The Maltese Falcon</u>, <u>October</u>

Alternative films: <u>My Man Godfrey</u> (Gregory La Cava), <u>His Girl Friday</u> (Howard Hawks), <u>The Freshman</u> (Sam Taylor and Fred Neumeyer), <u>Wild and Woolly</u> (John Emerson), <u>Battleship Potemkin</u> (Sergei Eisenstein), <u>Mother</u> (Vsevolod Pudovkin), <u>Mr. Hulot's Holiday</u> (Jacques Tati), <u>M</u> (Fritz Lang), <u>Othello</u> (Orson Welles), <u>Stray Dog</u> (Akira Kurosawa), <u>Psycho</u> (Alfred Hitchcock), <u>Jaws</u> (Steven Spielberg), <u>Pierrot le fou</u> (Jean-Luc Godard), <u>Back to the Future</u> (Robert Zemeckis), <u>El Mariachi</u> (Robert Rodriguez)

EXAMINATION QUESTIONS

> in the margin indicates a question suitable for use in either a pop quiz or an exam.

Multiple-choice Questions

An ordinary Hollywood film typically contains:

*   a.   800 to 1200 shots.

      b.   300 to 400 shots.

      c.   2000 to 2500 shots.

      d.   1500 to 1800 shots.

> Which of the following is <u>not</u> a type of transition from one shot to another?

      a.   A dissolve

*   b.   A glide

      c.   A wipe

      d.   A fade

In the scene of the gas-station explosion in <u>The</u>

<u>Birds</u>, the editing depends on:

        a. Strong graphic matching.

*   b. Point-of-view shots and graphic disconti-
            nuity.

        c. Brief dissolves to create a montage
            sequence.

        d. Systematic crossing of the axis of ac-
            tion.

Lev Kuleshov's discovery, termed the "Kuleshov
Effect," suggests that:

        a. Graphic matches usually enhance the
            narrative clarity of a scene.

        b. The spectator's center of attention
            should be kept close to the middle of the
            screen from one shot to the next.

*   c. Even if no establishing shot is shown,
            spectators will still assume that objects
            in separate shots are near each other.

        d. Spectators will tend not to notice edit-
            ing if matches on action and shot/reverse
            shot are consistently used.

"Cross-cutting":

*   a. Alternates between simultaneous shots in
            two separate spaces.

        b. Moves back and forth across the axis of
            action.

        c. Refers to flashbacks introduced by direct
            cuts rather than dissolves or fade-outs.

        d. Alternates long-shot views with close-
            ups.

> A temporal ellipsis in editing:

a.   Repeats an action.

b.   Shows parallel actions.

*   c.   Eliminates part of the action.

d.   Creates a smooth match on action.

"Overlapping editing":

a.   Refers to cutting away to action happen-
     ing elsewhere.

*   b.   Expands the scene by showing more than
          one view of the same action.

c.   Refers to placing a small portion of one
     strip of film over another in order to
     make a splice.

d.   Means the editing is so fast that the
     audience cannot see what is happening in
     the individual shots.

"Continuity editing" is:

a.   A method of rapidly editing on video as
     the film is being shot.

b.   Editing that creates a regular rhythm
     for a scene.

c.   Editing that becomes progressively more
     rapid during a scene.

*   d.   A system for keeping the spatial and
          temporal relations of a scene clear.

The "axis of action" is:

a.   An imaginary vertical line down the
     center of the screen around which the
     characters are placed to preserve graphic
     continuity.

*   b.   An imaginary line between the main charactors that determines where the camera should be placed to preserve continuity.

    c.   An imaginary line between the main character and the camera that determines where the camera should be placed for close-ups.

    d.   An imaginary line between the camera and the back of the set that determines where the camera should be placed for close-ups.

Which of the following is <u>not</u> a characteristic of the 180-degree system?

    a.   It keeps part of the background consistent from shot to shot.

    b.   It ensures constant screen direction from shot to shot.

*   c.   It ensures a temporal overlap from shot to shot.

    d.   It encourages not crossing the axis of action.

The opening scene of <u>The Maltese Falcon</u> contains examples of what type of editing?

    a.   Crosscutting

    b.   Montage sequence

    c.   Rhythmic cutting

*   d.   Shot/reverse shot

The 180-degree system is designed to:

*   a.   Ensure consistent screen direction across cuts.

    b.   Create smooth, unnoticeable matches on action across cuts.

c. Allow the camera to cut from action in one location to action elsewhere.

d. Avoid cutting in the middle of a camera movement to a static framing.

A "cheat cut" involves:

a. Crossing the axis of action but also matching on action.

b. "Cutting" the film in the camera so that actual splices are not needed.

c. Splicing together two shots taken from the same framing but with an ellipsis.

* d. A slight mismatch in the positions of mise-en-scene elements.

Crosscutting typically:

a. Provides a greater degree of continuity than shot/reverse shot does.

* b. Creates a less restricted knowledge of narrative events than other types of editing do.

c. Creates a more restricted knowledge of narrative events than other types of editing do.

d. Demands a great deal of matching on action.

In the continuity system, a montage sequence usually:

* a. Compresses a lengthy series of actions into a few moments.

b. Generates suspense during a last-minute-rescue situation.

c. Serves as a brief epilogue to the main

narrative.

    d.   Uses eyeline matching to guarantee clear spatial relations among shots.

Precise graphic matching in a narrative context is typical of the films of:

    a.   Stan Brakhage.

*   b.   Yasujiro Ozu.

    c.   Andy Warhol.

    d.   Bruce Conner.

> Which of the following is <u>not</u> a significant alternative to the techniques of the continuity system?

    a.   360-degree space

    b.   Nondiegetic inserts

    c.   Jump cuts

*   d.   Cheat cuts

> Which of the following is <u>not</u> characteristic of the editing in Sergei Eisenstein's <u>October</u>?

    a.   Graphic discontinuities

*   b.   Establishing shots

    c.   Crosscutting

    d.   Unclear temporal relations

True-False Questions

T <u>F</u> Films that use a great deal of editing are more "cinematic" than those that rely mostly on long takes.

> T <u>F</u> Film editing is usually a matter of cutting

together shots taken by multiple cameras on the set.

T <u>F</u> In order to create a smooth flow of narrative information, Hollywood films use detailed graphic matches for most cuts.

> <u>T</u> F In editing, rhythm depends upon the number of film frames in each shot.

T <u>F</u> An establishing shot is a close view that reveals a significant detail in the scene.

T <u>F</u> Skillful Hollywood editors try to time their cuts to come in the pauses between actors' lines.

> <u>T</u> F A scene's axis of action shifts as the characters move around the set.

> T <u>F</u> "Shot/reverse shot" refers to cutting across the axis of action.

> <u>T</u> F A camera movement is a common method of getting the framing across the axis of action.

<u>T</u> F Well-executed eyeline matches can eliminate the need for an establishing shot.

<u>T</u> F Flashbacks are the most common departure from a 1-2-3 temporal order in Hollywood continuity films.

<u>T</u> F Overlapping editing expands story duration.

Essay Questions

[Show a brief clip of about four shots three times, ideally twice at the beginning of the question and again about halfway through the allotted time. The shots should not be so short as to be impossible for the students to grasp them.] Discuss the most significant aspects of the editing in this short segment. Be sure to mention temporal, spatial, rhythmic, and graphic qualities in the cutting.

[Show, two or three times, a short conversation scene involving two or three characters that makes use of analytical editing, the 180-degree rules, and other principles of mainstream continuity editing.] Cite at least <u>three</u> techniques of continuity editing which can be found in this scene. What purposes are fulfilled by the devices you have singled out?

[You might make this a longer, comparative essay question by showing a second clip of about the same length but from a film made using editing techniques different from those of Hollywood. In that case, the same question could be used, but add "Describe at least three ways in which the editing in the second scene departs from the continuity tradition."]

CHAPTER NINE

SOUND IN THE CINEMA

Chapter Outline

The Powers of Sound
Fundamentals of Film Sound
 Acoustic Properties
 Selection, Alteration, and Combination
Dimensions of Film Sound
 Rhythm
 Fidelity
 Space
 Time
Functions of Film Sound: *A Man Escaped*
Notes and Queries
 The Power of Sound
 Acoustic Properties
 Silent Film versus Sound Film
 Film Music
 Dubbing and Subtitles

Teaching "Sound in the Cinema"

<u>The Purpose of the Chapter</u>

As with mise-en-scene, everyone notices sound while watching a film. But as we point out at the beginning of Chapter Nine, it is easy to assume that the people and things on the screen are making the sounds we hear, and that's all there is to it. Yet the sound track of a film can be elaborately designed, manipulated, and assembled, especially in this day of multiple-track recording and digital surround sound.

Chapter Nine aims to introduce the student to concepts and terms that permit analysis of the sonic experience.

<u>Teaching and Discussing Sound</u>

In our experience, the categories of sound

85

discussed in Chapter Nine can be more difficult to teach than the techniques discussed in the three previous chapters. The effects of costume motifs, high or low camera angles, jump cuts, and other stylistic traits are reasonably apparent on the screen. Such distinctions as simultaneous versus nonsimultaneous sound, external versus internal sound, and other categories used in Chapter Nine are more conceptual and hence more abstract and elusive for the students.

Thus it is important for your lectures to include examples that vividly demonstrate the power of these various possibilities of film sound. For the previous three chapters, the use of slides was often adequate to convey examples of mise-en-scene, cinematography, and editing. Here, if anywhere in the class, clips are essential. You can help your students master the terms used in Chapter Nine by choosing sequences with arresting instances of the use of, say, simultaneous diegetic sound (a character's interior monologue) or nonsimultaneous diegetic sound (a striking sound bridge). In presenting these clips, you could stress that the categories of sound are not just dry terms but ways of calling attention to vital differences among sonic techniques. And these technical differences affect how spectators respond to the film. A bit of practice can make students more comfortable with the types of sound laid out in Chapter Nine.

Again, of all the chapters in Film Art, this one would probably benefit the most from clips shown in a discussion session. Try showing a short clip, preferably from the film your students have already seen that week, then going through it bit by bit, sorting its various sounds into their appropriate categories (external simultaneous diegetic and so on). As you go, ask your students to suggest what functions these sounds play in the sequence and in the film as a whole. By simultaneously naming the types of sound and analyzing their functions, the students should come to understand the advantages of Chapter Nine's categories, as well as becoming more confident in using them.

In either lecture or discussion section, you

might try running a film with the image turned off but with the sound track audible. Try to choose a sequence in which the sounds are quite prominent and varied but which do not give obvious clues as to what is going on on the screen. (Dialogue scenes are usually not helpful for this sort of exercise. Animated cartoons that do not have much dialogue are particularly intriguing to students and can provide a vivid demonstration. They often have sounds that are exaggerated or lack fidelity to their purported sources. Some cartoon sound tracks provide relatively few clues as to what is happening on the screen.) Then show the same scene (or cartoon) with sound. This exercise could profitably be used to generate a discussion on how sound influences our expectations in a scene.

Assigning a Paper on Sound

The same basic topic described in the section on mise-en-scene in Chapter Six could be assigned, but with the students directed to write on one or more motifs of sound in a film.

SUGGESTED FILMS

Primary example from chapter: A Man Escaped

Alternative films: Mr. Hulot's Holiday (Jacques Tati), M (Fritz Lang), Le Million (René Clair), Providence (Alain Resnais), The Conversation (Francis Ford Coppola), Love Me Tonight (Rouben Mamoulian), Letter from Siberia (Chris Marker), Nashville (Robert Altman), Third Generation (Rainer Werner Fassbinder), The Hunt for Red October (John McTiernan), Distant Voices, Still Lives (Terence Davies), Do The Right Thing (Spike Lee)

(Note: The last three titles mentioned above will lose part of their value as examples if they are not reproduced in stereo.)

EXAMINATION QUESTIONS

> in the margin indicates a question suitable for use in either a pop quiz or an exam.

Multiple-choice Questions

The example from Chris Marker's <u>Letter from Siberia</u> used in <u>Film Art</u> demonstrates:

    a. The use of different images to accompany the same sound.

    b. The use of very precise, rhythmic synchronization.

*   c. The use of different sounds to accompany the same images.

    d. The use of multiple-track sound.

Which of the following is <u>not</u> an acoustic property of film sound?

    a. Loudness

    b. Pitch

    c. Timbre

*   d. Texture

A "dialogue overlap" means:

    a. Mixing sounds so that two or more characters speak at the same time.

    b. Creating realism by having one actor start to speak just before another finishes a line.

*   c. Continuing a line of dialogue over cuts during shot/reverse shot.

    d. A type of sound bridge that links one scene with the next.

The music in Truffaut's <u>Jules and Jim</u>:

    a.   Consists solely of a passage from a Beethoven string quartet played at wide intervals.

    b.   Comes entirely from diegetic sources within the scenes.

*   c.   Contains many motifs in waltz time that create comparisons among scenes.

    d.   Is considered innovatory in its use of jazz music.

> "Mickey Mousing" is:

    a.   The use of fast, cheerful music to accompany comic action.

    b.   The post-dubbing of sound effects created in a special studio.

*   c.   Very close synchronization of sound with the movement on the screen.

    d.   Redubbing objectionable language in preparing a film for television broadcast.

> In film sound, "fidelity" refers to:

    a.   Whether the sound comes from within the diegetic space of the story.

    b.   Whether the dialogue in a scene was actually spoken by the actors during shooting.

*   c.   Whether the type of sound heard seems appropriate to its source in the film.

    d.   Whether the lip synchronization has been done correctly.

Which of the following statements about diegetic

sound is <u>not</u> true?

     a. It can come from an offscreen or an onscreen source.

     b. It can come from a time later or earlier than the events occuring on the screen.

*   c. It can come from a source inside or outside the world of the narrative.

     d. It can be manipulated to lack fidelity to its source in the film.

The scene of the cavalry rescue in John Ford's <u>Stagecoach</u>:

*   a. Demonstrates how sound can call our attention to events happening offscreen.

     b. Shows that manipulation of a sound's fidelity can be used to create a striking transition.

     c. Greatly exaggerates the volume of the rifle shots to convey the characters' subjective reactions.

     d. Is an unusual case of a major action sequence being played with no music at all.

> The term for sound that represents a character's thoughts without him or her speaking aloud is:

     a. Mental sound.

*   b. Internal sound.

     c. Cognitive sound.

     d. Offscreen sound.

The prologue of Orson Welles's <u>The Magnificent Ambersons</u>:

*   a.   Contains a rare example of characters seeming to hear a nondiegetic narrator.

       b.   Contains a rare example of a nondiegetic onscreen narrator.

       c.   Consists of a lengthy soliloquy using internal diegetic sound.

       d.   Includes a scene where violins are used to simulate a woman's screams.

> Which factor does <u>not</u> affect sound perspective?

       a.   Timbre

       b.   Volume

       c.   Multichannel recording

*   d.   Synchronization

A "sound bridge" is:

       a.   A lightweight frame for quickly moving a microphone above the action while filming on location.

*   b.   Overlapping the sound of one scene into the next.

       c.   Boosting the volume of the music to make it more prominent than the voices or sound effects.

       d.   Transferring a sound from one channel to another in multichannel recording.

Alain Resnais's <u>Providence</u> and Francis Ford Coppola's <u>The Conversation</u> both contain examples of:

       a.   Major characters whose voices are heard but who never appear onscreen.

       b.   Scenes so dimly lit that sound becomes the main source of narrative information.

*   c.   Uses of sound that creates ambiguities.

    d.   The use of multichannel recording to
         create a dynamic sense of moving through
         space.

What is Robert Bresson noted for?

    a.   His invention of the THX program of
         certifying theater sound systems

*   b.   His exceptional skill in creating a
         complete interplay between sound and
         image in his films

    c.   For three decades he wrote all the music
         for Warner Bros.' cartoons

    d.   His skillful manipulation of diegetic
         sound for comic effect

The sound in A Man Escaped:

    a.   Creates the realistic atmosphere of a
         prison without conveying much narrative
         information.

    b.   Gives us little access to the hero's
         thoughts and thus makes his actions
         ambiguous.

*   c.   Often gives us narrative information we
         already know from the images.

    d.   Consists entirely of voice and sound
         effects with no music.

One important function of the sound in A Man
Escaped is:

*   a.   To call attention to small gestures and
         details.

    b.   To link parallel scenes with a complex
         variety of musical motifs.

c. To convey the differing psychological motivations of the German prison guards.

d. To convey the cheerful attitude the prisoners maintain despite their oppression.

The narration's range in A Man Escaped:

a. Moves freely among the prisoners to convey a sense of their solidarity.

b. Creates contrasts by moving systematically between scenes with the prisoners and scenes with their captors.

*   c. Gives us only as much information as the hero himself has.

d. Is carefully balanced between the hero and the boy who joins his escape effort.

The music in A Man Escaped consists entirely of:

a. A piano playing quietly under scenes of the hero working at his escape plan.

*   b. Passages from a Mozart mass suggesting the hero's comradeship with other prisoners.

c. Popular German songs of the World War II era played on the prison guards' radios.

d. The prisoners' singing French folk tunes as they express their resistance to their situation.

>   The scene from A Man Escaped illustrated and analysed in Film Art uses which sound technique?

a. An intrusion of a nondiegetic sound effect into an otherwise diegetic sound track

b. An exaggerated rise in volume to empha-

size the breathing and heartbeats of the
two fearful men

    c. The culmination of the musical motif that
emphasizes the trust between the two
cellmates

*   d. Movement back and forth between the
internal and external diegetic speech of
the hero

True-False Questions

> T F "Diegetic" sound is defined as sound that
comes from an onscreen source.

> T F To aid in synchronization, the sound tracks
of animated films are recorded after all the
images are completed.

T F The final battle scene of <u>Seven Samurai</u> uses
a dense mix of sound effects without music.

T F In adjusting the rhythm of the editing in
relation to the sound, the editor always
tries to avoid "cutting against" the dialogue.

> T F Sound effects are the most common kind of
nondiegetic sound.

T F The phrase "sound over" usually refers to
nondiegetic and internal diegetic sounds.

T F <u>A Man Escaped</u> contains diegetic narration by
the main character.

T F In <u>A Man Escaped</u>, sound motifs function iron-
ically to underline the other prisoners'
reluctance to help the hero escape.

Essay Questions

[Two or three times, show a brief clip that makes
varied use of sound.] In this clip, which sounds
are diegetic, and which are nondiegetic? Is

significant use made of offscreen sound? Cite at least two narrative functions of the sound in this extract.

[Two or three times, show a brief clip that makes significant and varied use of offscreen sound.] Discuss the most significant aspects of the use of offscreen sound in this clip. Be sure to specify each type of sound that is used. Discuss also the narrative functions of the offscreen sound.

[For a longer, more challenging question, add the following:] What are two different ways in which filmmakers can use offscreen space? Draw upon examples from Film Art, the lectures, and any of the films seen in this class.

[If you prefer not to show a clip, the following essay question could be substituted:]
Describe what offscreen sound is and two major ways it can be used. Illustrate your answer with specific examples from Film Art, the lecture, and any film seen for this class.

CHAPTER TEN

STYLE AS A FORMAL SYSTEM

Chapter Outline

Teaching "Style as a Formal System"

The Purpose of the Chapter

Chapter Ten functions as a summary of Chapters Six through Nine, which introduced the four basic types of film technique. In those chapters, the techniques had been analyzed in extended scenes or whole films, but only in isolation. For example, in Chapter Six we analyzed only the mise-en-scene in Our Hospitality, putting aside its cinematography and editing. Chapter Ten brings all the techniques together for the first time in detailed stylistic analyses of whole films. As we mentioned in the introduction to this instructor's manual, the most important purpose of Film Art is to teach students how to analyse whole films, not just recognize isolated techniques.

Moreover, the chapter seeks to show that the interaction of techniques shapes a film's overall style. Continuity editing requires certain standardized decisions about performance, framing, and lighting. The apotheosis of the diving sequence at the end of Olympia, Part 2 depends on the patterned cooperation of camera angle, music, and cutting. Welles's "deep focus" is a matter of cinematography and mise-en-scene. In turn, the cooperation of techniques works with the film's overall form to achieve particular effects.

Once the students have finished this chapter, they should be ready to analyze every aspect of a film on their own. They have been introduced to the different types of form that are used to shape whole films, and they know all the individual techniques that go into the making of the scene-by-scene progression of the film within that formal system.

"Style as a Formal System" as a Summary

Since this chapter is intended as a summary, you have a number of options in teaching it.

You may wish to show one of the films discussed in the chapter: a second showing of <u>Citizen Kane</u> or a screening of some of the films exemplifying nonnarrative form that you did not have time to show earlier. You may opt instead to show an entirely different film that uses all the techniques of film style and to hold a discussion session that allows students to ask questions on any aspect of filmic technique that may still puzzle them.

If your semester is organized in such a way that you give an exam about three-quarters of the way through your syllabus, you may opt to assign this chapter as a summary leading into that exam. You could then use it as an occasion for a review-and-question session.

Another alternative is to use this chapter as a lead-in to your assignment of a term paper. In this case, you could have a discussion session which concentrates on the film shown for the week, then ends with a short period in which your students can ask questions about the nature of the paper assignment.

Assigning a Paper on Film Style

In assigning a paper relating to Chapter Ten, there are two fundamental options. You can ask the students to choose a film and write only on its style, using the analyses in this chapter as models. Assuming, however, that you are assigning only one term paper in your class, you might prefer a more comprehensive analytical paper that includes the film's overall form (narrative or nonnarrative) as well. In that case, it would be helpful to have them read some or all of the Sample Analyses in Chapter Eleven and the appendix to that chapter, "Writing a Critical Analysis of a Film." Please see our comments on "Assigning an Analytical Paper" in the next chapter of this manual.

EXAMINATION QUESTIONS

Questions relating to this chapter are heavily dependent upon the film you choose to show. As we have suggested, this may be a good opportunity to give a comprehensive test on all four types of film technique and how they relate to style as a formal system. Alternatively, it might serve as a springboard into the students' analytical term paper.

CHAPTER ELEVEN

FILM CRITICISM: SAMPLE ANALYSES

Chapter Outline

The Purpose of the Sample Analyses

Throughout <u>Film Art</u>, we stress that students should study filmic techniques without isolating them from their contexts in the film as a whole. We encourage them not to take a single technique and interpret it in a rote way--as with the old overgeneralization that a high angle down on a character always means that he or she is weak. We stress that films are formal systems and that their various parts are interconnected. Each of the chapters on film form and style emphasizes that filmic techniques perform functions that the analyst can only understand by examining the film's unique formal system.

In keeping with this holistic approach, each

chapter on film form and technique contains at least one extended example, as with the examination of mise-en-scene in Our Hospitality (Chapter Six). Now, at the end of the chapter that examines the individual elements of film as an art form, we present a series of longer extended examples. Here not just a single technique, but all techniques, are analyzed across whole films.

Teaching the Sample Analyses

You can use the sample-analysis chapter in a variety of ways.

For example, you might teach the book's chapters in order, reserving some time toward the end of your class to show one or more of the films analyzed in Chapter Eleven, having the students read the relevant analyses. This would be a way of reviewing the material from the previous chapters, giving the students more practice in watching for camera movement, editing, and other techniques, as well as practicing how to recognize how these techniques function across a film.

If you want to challenge your students a bit more, you could have them read a sample analysis, watch the film on their own, show another film by the same director, and have them discuss it or write papers on it. Thus for example, they might read the analysis of Tokyo Story and then watch Yasujiro Ozu's Late Spring or An Autumn Afternoon, picking out the director's distinctive approach to narrative and film style for themselves. Similarly, a screening of Martin Scorsese's GoodFellas could lead to a discussion of the extent to which Film Art's analysis of the ideology of Raging Bull applies to GoodFellas as well.

Using another approach, you might show some of the films analyzed in Chapter Eleven interspersed through the semester. Thus Breathless might provide a good accompaniment to the editing or cinematography chapter, and you could assign the Breathless analysis along with that chapter.

Assigning an Analytical Paper

The sample analyses are equally intended for

use if you wish to assign a paper in which the students analyze a film for themselves. Some teachers do not show any of the films discussed in the sample analyses, but they assign their students to read many or all of them as models for their papers. The chapter also includes a section on "Writing a Critical Analysis of a Film," which could be read either before or after the students read the sample analyses themselves.

By the way, if you do assign a paper, it is a good idea to limit the students' choice of a film by giving them a short list of possible titles. For one thing, this guarantees that you will have seen all the films they analyze and will not end up having to watch a batch of new films in order to do your grading. For another, it reduces the prospect of bought papers or plagiarism from published sources. In addition, assigning a limited set of films prevents students from choosing the latest teenage-oriented hit. Assuming that the paper assignment comes late in the course, the students should be capable of dealing with classics and foreign films.

Ideally, the students should be able to see the films they are going to analyze at least twice projected on a screen, and then as many times as necessary on video. Thus if you know a local film society will be showing a suitable film more than once, you might include it on the list of possible paper topics. Similarly, if possible you might arrange to show a small selection of films two or more times each and then let students work with video. (In such circumstances, a choice of around three to five different films should be sufficient.)

As we mentioned in our general comments at the beginning, it is a good idea to keep photocopies of the best papers on file. If students want to improve their grades, reading excellent work by their peers often gives them concrete help.

CHAPTER TWELVE

FILM FORM AND FILM HISTORY

Chapter Outline

Teaching "Film Form and Film History"

The Purpose of the Chapter

The purpose of this chapter can best be described negatively. We do not intend Chapter Twelve to be a brief survey of the entirety of film history. This would be impossible in an introductory aesthetics textbook. Rather, this chapter is a sketch of the historical highlights of film form and style. It is designed to do nothing more than place some of the films students will have seen in an historical perspective and to prepare them to move on to a class devoted specifically to film history.

After reading this chapter, the students should have a grasp of the outline of the major movements and trends in the history of the cinema. Even if they never take another film course, they should be able to recognize such important trends as German Expressionism and Italian Neorealism. The final portion on "The New Hollywood and Independent Filmmaking" to some extent has an additional purpose. It also points out to them that the era in which they themselves live is part of film history. In it we aim to acquaint them with the current practices of the film industry, as well as with the types of movies being made--issues that affect them directly.

Teaching Film History

Chapter Twelve is designed to give you flexibility in integrating it into your course. Some teachers present this chapter as part of a separate unit on film history, reserving time at the end of the course for that purpose. The students can be assigned to read the entire chapter, with one or more historically important films being shown in class.

Another approach is to chose a set of films to be shown throughout the semester, in relation to the previous eleven chapters, that are also mentioned in Chapter Twelve as historically important. Thus The Cabinet of Dr. Caligari could be shown the week that Chapter Six, on mise-en-scene, is assigned. That week's assignment could also include the section from Chapter Twelve on German Expressionism. Similarly, Breathless could be shown during the unit on cinematography, with Chapter Seven and the section on the French New Wave in Chapter Twelve being assigned (and optionally the analysis of the film in Chapter Eleven). Thus one could build a syllabus that teaches the various aesthetic aspects of film and the outline of film history in parallel. (You might take a slightly different approach by using this same tactic but assigning the students to read the entire history chapter at the beginning of the semester, so that they understand the historical context of each film as it is shown.)

A bibliography of basic historical sources that may be of use in preparing your lectures follows the "Examination Questions" section.

EXAMINATION QUESTIONS

> in the margin indicates a question suitable for

use in either a pop quiz or an exam.

Multiple-choice Questions

Eadweard Muybridge contributed to the invention of the cinema by:

* a. Using a row of several cameras to photograph a moving horse.

    b. Building a camera with twelve lenses to photograph a moving train.

    c. Inventing a flexible film stock as a substitute for photographic glass plates.

    d. Devising a revolving shutter that could create multiple exposures of an animal's movement on a single glass plate.

Étienne-Jules Marey contributed to the invention of the cinema by:

    a. Creating a film that made very short photographic exposures possible.

* b. Building a motion-analysis camera that used a strip of flexible film.

    c. Fastening a series of small drawings together to make the first animated film.

    d. Inventing a special claw mechanism to pull the film through the camera.

Louis and Auguste Lumière:

    a. Developed an extremely popular peep-show machine, the Kinetoscope, for exhibiting early short films.

    b. Analyzed animals' movements using an early cinema camera of their own invention.

* c. Held one of the earliest presentations of

films projected on a screen.

    d.   Were assistants to Thomas A. Edison and invented the first film camera.

> Georges Méliès:

    a.   Built a small film studio called the Black Maria that rotated to catch sun-light.

    b.   Was one of the major filmmakers of the Brighton School.

    c.   Invented the first successful cinema camera, the Cinétographe.

*   d.   Built a glass-walled studio in order to use sunlight for filming indoors.

Thomas A. Edison formed the Motion Picture Patents Company:

    a.   Because he felt film was a passing fad and he wished to sell his patents.

    b.   In order to foster inventions relating to film.

*   c.   In an attempt to control companies competing with him in the American market.

    d.   Hoping to buy up patents of successful film cameras invented in England and Europe.

> For which of the following was D. W. Griffith not responsible?

    a.   Popularizing cross-cutting for rescue scenes

    b.   Directing Intolerance

    c.   Filming his actors in relatively close framings to catch subtle facial expressions

* d. Inventing the close-up

Typical characteristics of German Expressionist films include:

    a. Rapid editing, frequent point-of-view shots, and location shooting.

*   b. Distorted mise-en-scene and narratives based on the fantasy or horror genres.

    c. Restrained acting, and fluid camera movements, and avoidance of continuity editing.

    d. Many close framings to create subtle psychological studies of a small group of characters.

Which of the following factors did not contribute to the decline of German Expressionism?

    a. Increasing competition from foreign films

    b. The departure of actors and directors to Hollywood

    c. Increasingly high film budgets that led to financial problems

*   d. Censorship imposed by the Nazis

Typical characteristics of French Impressionist films include:

    a. A largely static camera, symbolic non-diegetic inserts, and amateur actors.

    b. Frame stories, dynamic camera angles, and adherence to continuity editing conventions.

*   c. Superimpositions, fast rhythmic editing,

and psychologically-based narratives.

    d. Settings that reflect the characters'
        mental states and acting that uses jerky,
        exaggerated movements.

Which of the following factors did <u>not</u> contribute
to the decline of French Impressionism?

    a. The films proved difficult to export.

    b. The films appealed primarily to an elite
        audience.

    c. Big-budget failures late in the movement

*   d. Many major filmmakers departed for Holly-
        wood.

Which of the following was a serious problem faced
by the Soviet film industry after the 1917 Revolu-
tion?

*   a. Shortages of film equipment and raw
        stock

    b. The shutdown of the State School of
        Cinema Art and the resulting lack of a
        new generation of directors

    c. Lenin's New Economic Policy hindered the
        growth of the film industry.

    d. Lenin declared, "Of all the arts, for us
        the cinema is the least important," and
        offered little support.

Which of the following is <u>not</u> a theoretical view
of film held by one of the Soviet Montage directors?

    a. Pudovkin believed that shots were put
        together like bricks to build a sequence.

    b. Vertov compared the camera lens to a
        "cinema eye" recording reality.

    c. Kuleshov wrote that dissolves should
        replace cuts to smoothe the film's flow.

    d. Eisenstein declared that the editing
        should create conflict and a jolt for
        the spectator.

>   Which studio and film listed below introduced the
    first commercially successful method accompanying
    films with recorded sound?

    a. Paramount's <u>Applause</u>

    b. MGM's <u>The Good Earth</u>

*   c. Warner Bros.' <u>Don Juan</u>

    d. Fox's <u>Sunrise</u>

The 1930s introduction of Technicolor encouraged
which stylistic trend in Hollywood films?

    a. The lower levels of light needed for
        Technicolor were adapted to create dark,
        atmospheric "film noirs" in black and
        white.

    b. The realistic colors rendered by Techni-
        color led to extensive location shooting.

    c. The enormous Technicolor cameras made all
        but short panning movements impossible,
        creating a brief vogue for adapted stage
        plays.

*   d. The greater levels of light needed for
        Technicolor permitted filmmakers to
        experiment with deep-focus shots in black
        and white.

>   Which of the following is <u>not</u> a typical trait of
    Italian Neorealism?

        a. Mixing of professional actors with nonac-
            tors

b. Loosely constructed narratives with ambiguity and open endings

* c. Use of the three-point lighting system on location

   d. Shooting scenes silent and postsynchronizing the sound

A major factor in the decline of Italian Neorealism was:

   a. The economic decline of the Italian film industry in the 1950s.

   b. The departure of several key filmmakers to work in Hollywood.

   c. The rise of other, more popular European film movements to supply American art theaters.

* d. Censorship and other governmental pressures.

The young directors of the French New Wave got their start:

   a. As critics for <u>Cahiers du cinéma</u>, which they founded as a forum for attacking classical Hollywood cinema.

   b. As critics who studied under older French filmmakers and were able to work their way up in the studios.

* c. By borrowing money to make short films and features using location shooting.

   d. By forming a filmmaking cooperative, the "Société des Auteurs" and renting a small studio.

Which of the following traits is <u>not</u> typical of French New Wave films?

a. Casual humor and references to other films

b. Many tracking, panning, and handheld camera movements

c. Shooting in real buildings using available light

* d. Exaggeratedly melodramatic plots and frequent criticism of the French government

Which of these circumstances allowed the rise of the new generation of younger filmmakers, or "movie brats," in Hollywood during the 1970s?

a. A return to the classic studio system of Hollywood's "Golden Age" of the 1930s and 1940s, with directors placed under long-term contract

b. The enormous box-office success of youth-oriented films, or "youthpix" during the late 1960s and early 1970s

c. Hollywood producers' decision to hire directors who had proven themselves with successful television series

* d. The box-office failures of big-budget films of the 1960s and youth-oriented films of the early 1970s

Which of the following factors did not differentiate such "movie brats" as Francis Ford Coppola, Brian De Palma, and Martin Scorsese from earlier directors?

a. They attended film schools and learned the history of the cinema.

* b. They were the first generation to be heavily influenced by music videos.

c.   They self-consciously borrowed from earlier Hollywood films.

d.   They greatly admired the European art cinema of the 1950s and 1960s.

> Which of the following factors has <u>not</u> had a significant impact on recent Hollywood cinema?

a.   European and Australian directors

b.   Women filmmakers

c.   Directors moving over from independent filmmaking

*   d.   Emigré directors seeking work after the break-up of the Soviet Union

True-False Questions

> <u>T</u> F   Edwin S. Porter made <u>The Great Train Robbery</u>, an early forerunner of the classical American film.

T <u>F</u>   The basic techniques of Hollywood continuity filmmaking first appeared in the 1920s.

T <u>F</u>   German Expressionism arose as an attempt to rebuild the German film industry, which had declined enormously during World War I.

<u>T</u> F   One of the main kinds of films made in Germany after World War I was the historical epic.

<u>T</u> F   The French Impressionist filmmakers worked largely within the mainstream commercial film industry.

> T <u>F</u>   The most important Surrealist films of the 1920s were made in England.

T <u>F</u>   Most Soviet Montage films were made by directors who had begun in the industry during or before World War I.

111

> T F The Soviet Montage movement declined primari-
       ly due to pressure from the Stalinist govern-
       ment.

> T F The earliest commercially successful sound
       system involved synchronizing phonograph
       records with a projected image.

  T F The introduction of sound and color radically
       changed the classical Hollywood approach to
       constructing narratives.

  T F Virtually all of the Italian Neorealist
       directors were young film critics who made
       their first films just after World War II.

> T F French New Wave films continued the experi-
       mentation with plot construction begun by the
       Italian Neorealists.

  T F From the beginning, the French film industry
       was hostile to the New Wave and eventually
       contributed to its decline.

> T F The shared interests and training of the
       younger generations of American filmmakers
       have made the "New New Hollywood" a unified
       stylistic movement.

Essay Questions

What does a film movement consist of? Give two
specific examples from Film Art, lectures, and
films seen in class.

[This question assumes you have shown a film
relating to one of the nine sections of Chapter
Twelve.] Cite at least two ways in which [film
title] exemplifies the [   ] movement?
Give specific examples from the film and from the
discussion of [film movement] in lecture and in
Film Art.

PART THREE

MAKING SLIDES/USEFUL ADDRESSES

MAKING SLIDES FROM FILM AND VIDEO IMAGES

Although <u>Film Art</u> is heavily illustrated with frame enlargements that exemplify the techniques discussed, you may wish to make slides for showing your students additional examples. Moreover, slides can be useful during examinations, allowing you to leave an image on the screen and ask students to write about its visual style.

Most of the illustrations in <u>Film Art</u> are frame enlargements photographed from the strip of film itself. Some film textbooks depend instead on publicity photographs taken on the set during shooting. The disadvantage of publicity photographs is that they do not show the film image <u>as it actually appears on the screen</u>. We recommend the use of slides taken in the same way the illustrations in <u>Film Art</u> were--from film frames.

Some universities and colleges have a technical support staff available to make slides for teachers. Many do not, however, and you may be in a position of needing to make your own slides. Here we will outline some methods for photographing from 35mm prints, 16mm prints, and video images. Some of this terminology may sound complicated to those who are not experienced with photography, but the staff of your local photographic store should be able to give you information and advice.

All these methods require a camera that uses 35mm still film and has through-the-lens metering. That is, the camera has some sort of dial or gauge visible alongside the image field when one looks through the viewfinder. The camera must also have manual controls for the f-stop settings and speed of exposure. This is because film frames vary considerably in brightness, and the exposure needs to be adjusted from shot to shot and film to film.

Photographing Directly from 35mm and 16mm Prints

The ideal way to photograph slides is to take them directly from 35mm prints of films, since that will render the best visual quality. (We have done this for most of the stills illustrating

Film Art.) In practice, teachers are often using 16mm copies. Similar procedures are used to photograph both. For the first methods we will describe, the film needs to be on an editing table (e.g., a Steenbeck) or on a pair of rewinds.

In order to photograph from a strip of film, you need to be able to hold the film steady in front of the camera lens and to light it from behind. You also need a lens capable of focusing on a very small object very close up--usually a macro lens or a bellows system or a combination of the two.

As of this writing, Canon is the only company that makes a device specifically designed to hold a strip of 35mm film for reproduction: the Canon Duplicator 35. (It may soon be taken out of the Canon catalogue, but you may be able to track one down through your local camera store.) It has a small hinged gate that clamps the film in place with small metal strips that touch only the sprocket-hole portions at the sides. The Duplicator 35 is screwed onto the front of the Canon Auto Bellows. A Canon FD50/3.5 Macro lens is required for the proper focus and magnification. A double release cable is necessary for triggering the shutter. These pieces of equipment do not fit any type of camera other than a Canon. When shooting from the Duplicator 35, the camera body must be swivelled 90 degrees to the side, so that it is vertical rather than the usual horizontal.

Once this equipment is assembled, you place a lamp with a photoflood bulb at a small distance behind the Duplicator 35 as a light source. Various types of photoflood bulbs are available, but the smallest, at 250 watts, is bright enough for this purpose. (Be careful not to get the film strip too near the photoflood, as the heat could warp or melt it.) Your slide film should be color balanced with the photoflood bulb, because if it is not, your slides will come out with a blue or orange cast. (This is true even if you are shooting from a black-and-white print.) Usually this would mean using a film balanced for tungsten light (e.g., Kodak Ektachrome 160T or Fujichrome 64T), with the photoflood bulb at 3200 degrees Kelvin. (See illustration.)

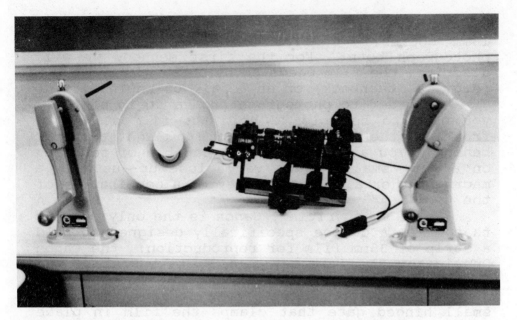

The Canon Duplicator 35, lamp, and rewinds

Once the film is in the Duplicator 35 and focused, use the camera's light meter to determine the correct exposure and take the photo. You will only be able to change the shutter speed, not the f-stop, since the lens is attached to the bellows rather than to the camera. If the shot is very bright, you should shoot at a half to a full stop over what the meter tells you is the correct exposure; conversely, a very dark shot needs to be underexposed slightly. (This procedure is similar to the real-life situation of photographing a person against a bright sky; in that case, you would also overexpose so that the face did not come out too dark.) If the shot is important, you should consider "bracketing" exposures, that is, taking two or three shots at different shutter speeds.

Until recently, Canon also made a smaller Duplicator 16 for 16mm film. It is essentially used in the same way as the Duplicator 35, but it requires a Canon Macrophoto 35mm Lens. Again, your camera store may be able to find these pieces of equipment still in stock in large photo supply houses or warehouses. This works in the same way as the Duplicator 35. (See illustration.)

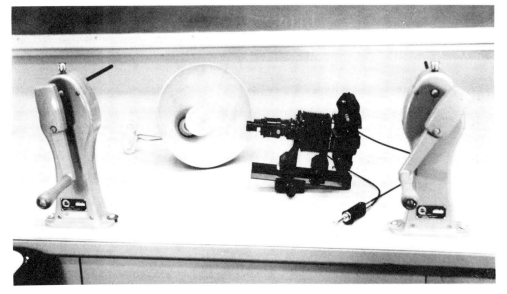

The Canon Duplicator 16, lamp, and rewinds

    A cheaper and simpler solution is to use a
slide duplicator to make frame enlargements. This
type of equipment is designed to let people make
copies of slides using the same sort of back
lighting described above. Slide duplicators are
basically macro-lens systems with a small hinged
door that clamps the slide in front of the lens.
(The disadvantage of most slide duplicators in
comparison with the Canon systems is that they
tend to use mediocre lenses that yield somewhat
less sharp results, especially from 16mm.) Un-
fortunately, the hinges on slide duplicators are
designed for horizontal slides, not for the vertical strip of images on a roll of movie film.
Hence on some models the hinges are attached at
the bottom center of the swinging door and prevent
the insertion of the film. It is possible to get
a machinist to place the hinges at the side,
transforming the slide duplicator into a film
duplicator.
    On some slide duplicators, however, the
hinged portion slides off, leaving a flat, rectangular plate with a rectangular opening on the end
of the duplicator tube. It is then simple to lay
the strip of film you want to photograph across a
light box, place the end of the duplicator on it,

117

set the f-stop and exposure time, and shoot the frame from above. (See illustration; the small object to the right of the light box is the slide holder, here detached from the duplicator.)

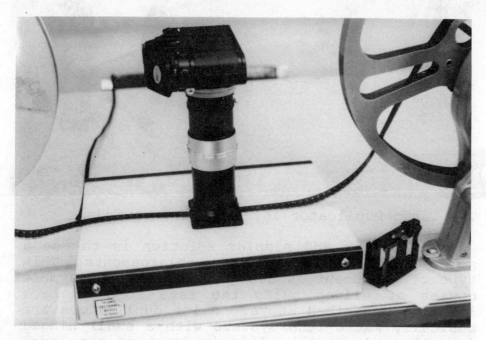

Camera, zoom slide duplicator, light box, rewinds

Again, the light source must be balanced for the kind of color film you are using. Most commercially available light boxes are balanced for tungsten, but it is best to check.

   The type of slide duplicator illustrated has a zoom feature (intended to allow home photographers to enlarge portions of their slides). When zoomed out, the lens of the duplicator will photograph 35mm frames; when zoomed in to full magnification, it blows 16mm frames up to fill most of the slide area. If you are filming 16mm and wish to show two frames around a cut, the zoom slide duplicator allows you to zoom out and fit both in the same slide. Currently zoom slide duplicators are distributed under a variety of names, including Rokunar, Spirotone, and Coast. Many good camera stores keep such duplicators in stock.

When purchasing or ordering a slide duplicator, explain to the sales person what you need it for and make sure that it will serve your purpose. The main things to avoid are 1) a slide duplicator with no zoom feature and 2) one without a detachable slide holder.

There are many types of slide duplicators, and camera equipment models change frequently, so you may be able to find some other type that will serve the same purpose.

Photographing an Image Projected on a Screen

If you cannot get access to equipment for taking slides directly off the filmstrip, you may wish to try taking them off a screen while a 16mm film is being projected. (The visual quality of the slides will be considerably less sharp and detailed than with the methods just described, but some practice should allow you to get usable images.) Place the projector fairly high and angled down just slightly. Attach your camera to a tripod and raise it until the camera is just underneath the projector beam. The lowest-numbered f-stop should be used to maximize the light entering the lens. You will need to read the camera's light meter to determine the proper f-stop setting, which will depend on how bright the projector beam is and how reflective the screen is. The exposure time should ideally be one-thirtieth of a second; a longer time would expose two or more frames on the same slide, while a shorter one would risk photographing nothing but the dark interval between frames. (If you have a freeze-frame projector, you have more flexibility in adjusting for the proper exposure.) The slide film you use should be balanced for tungsten.

Making Slides from a Video Monitor

If you do not have access to 35mm or 16mm prints, you can make slides from a television screen. They will have disadvantages: the pattern of pixels will be apparent when they are projected, and virtually all your slides will show at least a slight scan line. (A scan line is a diagonal dark strip that shows the path of the guns in the picture tube passing across the back of the screen to create the video image.) Still, video images can be reasonably acceptable for lectures and presentations.

To make slides from video, set your camera on a tripod and center it in front of the monitor screen, just far enough away so that the entire image is visible through the viewfinder. The room should be as dark as possible, with no lights or windows reflecting off the screen; these will show up annoyingly in your slide. You should use a slide film balanced for daylight (e.g., Kodak Ektachrome 400).

The best video source for taking slides is a laserdisc. If it is CAV or if your laserdisc player can freeze CLV frames, you can halt the image and set the exposure time for exactly what the meter reads as optimal. With a longer exposure, you can almost eliminate the scan line. In shooting from a moving video image, you need to shoot at one-thirtieth of a second; any slower, and you will record two or more frames, creating blur and "ghost" images. A thirtieth of a second is adequate for most video images, but dark shots will tend to be underexposed. Use the camera's built-in meter to determine the proper f-stop setting that will allow you to shoot at a thirtieth of a second. Dark shots are particularly tricky on video, often coming out nearly black. Thus you may wish to take two or three exposures at different f-stop settings when you shoot such scenes.

Mounting Your Slides

No matter which slide-making method you use, you should ask the photographic laboratory that develops your slides not to cut or mount them. This is because all these methods leave broad black bands between the film images (rather than the usual narrow bands that separate regular slide images), and these trigger the automatic cutters used by laboratories. Thus the slides often come back to you with the image far off center or even cropped. If you have them left uncut, the slides

120

will then be returned to you as a long strip which you can cut apart with ordinary scissors and mount in plastic slide mounts available from photography stores.

A ballpoint pen can be used to label the slide mounts.

USEFUL ADDRESSES

The Society for Cinema Studies

The main national organization for film teachers and graduate students is the Society for Cinema Studies. It holds an annual conference and publishes a quarterly, refereed journal, Cinema Journal. The address for applying for membership changes every two years as new secretaries are elected; for the current address, check the inside back cover of a recent issue of Cinema Journal in your school library. Subscriptions to the journal are available from:

> **Cinema Journal**
> University of Texas Press Journals
> Box 7819
> Austin TX   78713-7819
> Phone (512) 471-4531
> Fax (512) 320-0668
> email journal_orders@utpress.ppb.utexas.edu

Companies Distributing 16mm and 35mm Films

Canyon Cinema
2324 Third Street, Suite 338
San Francisco CA   94107
(415) 626-2255

Film-Makers' Cooperative
175 Lexington Avenue
New York NY 10016
(212) 889-3820
(Mainly experimental and alternative films)

Films Incorporated
5547 North Ravenswood Avenue
Chicago IL   60640-1199
800-323-4222, ext. 42

Kino International Corporation
333 West 39th Street, Suite 503

New York NY   10018
(212) 629-6880
Fax (212) 714-0871

Kit Parker Films
P.O. Box 16022
Monterey CA   93942-6022
800-538-5838
(408) 393-0303
Fax (408) 393-0304

Milestone Film & Video
275 West 96th Street, Suite 28C
New York NY   10025

Circulating Film Library
The Museum of Modern Art
11 West 53rd Street
New York NY   10019
(212) 708-9530

New Yorker Films
16 West 61st Street
New York NY   10023
(212) 247-6110
Fax (212) 307-7855

The Samuel Goldwyn Company
10203 Santa Monica Boulevard
Los Angeles CA   90067
(310) 284-9278

Swank Motion Pictures, Inc.

New York office (for Connecticut, Delaware, the
District of Columbia, Maine, Maryland, Massachu-
setts, New Hampshire, New Jersey, New York, Penn-
sylvania, Rhode Island, Vermont, Virginia):

    350 Vanderbilt Motor Parkway
    Hauppauge NY   11787-4305
    800-876-3344
    (516) 434-1560
    Fax (516) 434-1574

Chicago office (for northern Illinois, Indiana,

Michigan, Ohio, Wisconsin):

    910 Riverside Drive
    Elmhurst IL   60126-4967
    800-876-3330
    (708) 833-0061
    Fax (708) 833-0096

St. Louis (for southern Illinois and all other states):

    201 South Jefferson Avenue
    St. Louis MO   63103-2579
    800-876-5577
    (314) 534-6300
    Fax (314) 289-2192